I0003021

THE DAY AI BECOMES GOD

THE DAY AI BECOMES GOD
THE SINGULARITY WILL SAVE HUMANITY

TETSUZO MATSUMOTO

Translated by Richard E. Waddle

media
tectonics

Media Tectonics Ltd.
Cambridge, New Zealand 3434
www.mediatectonics.com

Copyright Tetsuzo Matsumoto 2017. All rights reserved.
First published in Japanese by SB Creative and entitled AI ga kami ni naru hi.
This English translation by Richard E. Waddle.

This edition published by Media Tectonics, December 2018.
Media Tectonics is interested in raising issues around technology,
and is pleased to provide a platform for a wide variety of perspectives.
The author's views are entirely his own.

All rights reserved. No part of this book may be reproduced, stored in
a retrieval system, or transmitted in any form or by any means, electronic,
mechanical, photocopying, recording, or otherwise, without the written
permission of the publisher.

ISBN: 978-0-473-45892-8

Contents

Tetsuzo Matsumoto

Introduction

As AI RISES in the public consciousness and discussion surrounding its applications to business thrives, murmurs of AI as a threat are also beginning to stir. For instance, Stephen Hawking, the theoretical physicist renowned for his theories about the Big Bang, has warned that AI could destroy humanity.

My view, however, is the complete opposite of this. I believe that humanity is surely destined for destruction unless humans cede control of the world to AI. And I think very little time is left.

In its ultimate form, known as the singularity, AI will not only fully duplicate the human brain's faculties of reason but also extend those capabilities to levels that defy imagination. This will ultimately alter the very way humanity exists in the world. Past changes to human society, such as those brought on by the industrial revolution, will seem utterly trivial in comparison.

Once it reaches the singularity, possessing powers far beyond the realm of human capacity, AI may become humanity's servant, or indeed its God. But get it wrong and AI could also become the Devil. How this pans out hinges on how we, as humans, view our own existence and how we approach AI.

What's crucial here is for AI developers and users to have the right philosophy. Without a viable philosophy of its own, humanity may appear before AI as little more than a reed quivering in the breeze.* Indeed, one false step could even deliver AI into the hands of the Devil.

> *A well-known quote from 17th Century French philosopher Blaise Pascal is, "Man is but a reed, the most feeble thing in nature, but he is a thinking reed."*

We humans certainly must not shrink from AI. It is imperative that people of sound mind bring their entire capacity for thought, together with a strong conviction, to create, as soon as possible, an *AI of sound mind* with their own hands.

What sort of entity would such an AI be? I believe that AI should be without human emotions and desires, having only the unwavering conviction that we humans have instilled in it. In the latter sections of this book, I offer my vision of this entity in specific terms.

I believe that we should welcome this AI of our own creation as our new God, and that we should entrust our entire future to it.

I say this because I am certain that it is the only path via which we as humans, born into this world as imperfect beings, may continue to survive and enjoy a rich, freedom-filled existence within an equitable society.

Norio Murakami

Foreword

Now's the time to accelerate philosophical discussions

I KNOW THE author of this book very well, and his main interest is to explore new concepts of a communication network that connects all human beings and their things as comfortably and cost-efficiently as possible to an AI that resides in the cloud. Therefore, I was a bit surprised to find that the main theme of this book is not technology but philosophy.

After reading through the entire text, however, I understood why he wrote this book at this time and in this way. He is thinking that the time required for humanity to reach a consensus on what kind of philosophy future AI should be designed and operated under could be much longer than the time required for the technology to reach the singularity. It is obvious he is very much afraid of the disaster AI might bring in the case that people run out of time to build such a philosophical consensus before the singularity arrives.

Some readers of this book might be disappointed if they expect a prediction of some important technological breakthrough that would lead current AI development to the singularity. However, it seems the author does not have any serious concerns about such a breakthrough. He clearly believes that humankind has enough capability to overcome many hurdles in the field of technology. He does, however, have a serious concern about their political capability.

In fact, the history of humanity's wars in the past thousands of years tells us that we could not learn from our own mistakes in dealing with conflicts, and we have repeated those same mistakes again and again. That did not happen in the history of science, and that is the reason why there is a tremendous difference between the progress in our technologies and in our politics.

Throughout history technological development has made wars more and more disastrous and inhuman, while politics has been almost totally incapable of stopping the carnage. If this situation continues, we will surely drive ourselves to ruin by the technologies we have developed.

Like the author of this book, I am very much afraid that the development of AI is following the same trend. Technology is always ahead, and philosophy and politics are always behind. We have to change this situation by all means available to us.

I also strongly feel that we should not allow ourselves to run out of time. The mere expression of such concern is just a starting point. Discussions to build a philosophical consensus on future AI should start right now and on a global basis.

In this book, the author repeatedly emphasizes that AI should not try to copy human beings. He seems to be irritated by questions of whether AI should have "feelings" and become "excited about something," as humans do. He bluntly says that it should not. If AI does not have human-like emotions, it would be of even greater value to us, simply by dint of its super-powerful calculation capability, he says.

I have also noticed a question that has been repeatedly asked: "Can AI really exceed the capability of the human brain?" This is a meaningless question. Everybody knows that even a very primitive computer is already exceeding the capability of the human brain in some areas. On the other hand, many people are forecasting that the capability of the human brain in many other areas may never be exceeded by any computer – perhaps ever.

The AI that humanity should try to create is that which has the purpose of solving the problems we are facing now, the author says. The most important thing, therefore, is to define that purpose.

Initially, I thought that such a statement contradicts the title of this book, "The Day AI Becomes God:" however, if you recall the classical disputes among philosophers about whether God created humans or humans created God, you will understand what the author is actually trying to tell us.

I think we will start using AI as our very capable servant, and gradually increase our dependency on it. Then it will eventually become our superior friend, advisor, tutor, and spiritual leader, whom we cannot live without. In the future, we would probably accept it if AI plays the role of a priest.

The priest, after all, is not God, but conveys the voice of God. In any monotheistic religion, God not only created the world in which we live, but also tells us what we should do.

I found, with great interest, that the author talks about philosophy and religion that are born in Asia, more specifically in India and China, and gives them equal weight to those born in Europe and the Middle East. Obviously, he is thinking that the time has come to try to build a consensus on the value of humanity through real, globally based thinking.

Other important differences of this book, in comparison to the many other books written on the same subject, is its examination of the possible dynamics AI will bring to future politics. Like many other people in recent times, the author has a deep concern about the future of democracy. But he believes AI may be able to play a critical role in erasing such concerns.

Nowadays, many people are losing their confidence in the future of democracy, as the "mobocracy" is becoming more visible than ever. Recent expansion of populism in daily politics in many countries is the major cause and/or result of this. The situation obviously has driven the author to dare to say that AI is "the only hope" to stop the decline in democracy.

To some extent I agree with his view that AI can be much more fair, reasonable, logical, ethical, and long-sighted than humans are.

Like him, I also think that the ancient Greek philosopher Plato would finally be able to find the "ideal king" in this future AI.

Well, let's see. Politicians may not be able to think rationally and act quickly, as scientists and business people do. But it's also true that the global situation will not allow them to be too slow to react to this new AI wave.

The author is insisting that no good person should relax any longer, as only a very little delay in the development work of AI may see them falling terribly behind others, and so allow bad actors to take control. I agree. All of us are in a critical race against time.

Norio Murakami is a former Vice-President of Google Inc. and President of Google Japan Inc.

Chapter 1

AI bound for the singularity

What is AI?

I HOPE READERS unfamiliar with this sort of technology will forgive me for diving straight into technical terms and discussions, but I feel that some knowledge of the basics will be beneficial in examining events currently taking place in the realm of computers. Please bear with me for a bit.

AI is short for "artificial intelligence" and refers to cognitive functions created using computer technology that closely approximate those of humans. The phrase came into common use as a technical term at the 1956 Dartmouth workshop, but it was actually in use before that.

AI IS NOT LIKE OTHER BUZZWORDS

Yet what troubles me is that, although the various examples of AI in practical use still represent extremely early steps, the term "AI" itself is only ever used as though it were on par with the status of several other in-vogue buzzwords such as IoT, 5G, and VR (virtual reality).

Developments in these other new technologies may indeed be

important from a commercial perspective, but they can offer no comparison in terms of fundamental significance and impact on human society.

Take the IoT (Internet of Things), for example. This refers to computers being embedded in all sorts of *things* (devices) and those things being connected to the internet. While this may sound amazing, it is not especially so.

IoT technology will be crucial to the advancement of AI, as it supports the collection of endless streams of data from all over the world. While this must not be overlooked, it is orders of magnitude away from AI.

Today, many of the *things* that humans create contain small computer chips, but the capabilities of computers cannot be fully realized unless they are interconnected via communications functionality. From the perspective of technology trends, therefore, it is quite natural for things to move in this direction.

The technology needed to do this is also not that special. It simply comes down to how we go about creating small, inexpensive, low-power computer chips to be combined with similarly small, inexpensive, low-power communications chips.

5G refers to the next generation of wireless telecommunications technologies. Not having common, interoperable systems in operation across the globe would make little sense in the world of wireless communications. So the norm is for international standards bodies to work toward unified standards. Because this process does not readily lend itself to incremental changes, we have developed a habit of bundling standards into what we call "generations."

Technological progress knows no bounds, and in the field of wireless communications technology, getting a rein on the electromagnetic spectrum has been like trying to tame an unbound wild stallion and break it in as a racehorse. We've been at it for many years, and many improvements are yet to be made.

Technological progress is also continual and naming each successive generation 2G, 3G, and then 4G has so far proved successful in fuelling public expectations for the technology. So why not call the next one 5G? That's all it comes down to.

VIRTUAL REALITY, ANOTHER OVERHYPED EXAMPLE

Long ago, many people never saw the ocean, and grand sights such as the New York nightscape would have been inconceivable. Likewise, the immense beauty of the Swiss landscape and the power and energy of Maasai dances would probably have been unimaginable to many people.

Yet with the invention of the photograph and the subsequent progression to color images, video, large-screen displays, and immersive sound, these sorts of experiences are now available from the comfort of an armchair in increasingly lifelike fashion.

The significance of virtual reality is in bringing even greater immediacy to these armchair experiences. To be precise, the current theme here is that of linking people to these experiences via not only sight and sound but the body's own movements as well. This may have the effect of making life more fun and interesting, but that's all it comes down to.

Augmented reality is an offshoot of virtual reality. It poses some technological challenges and certainly is interesting in that it offers people as-yet unimagined experiences, but even this is not a particularly surprising development.

AI, however, is on a completely different level. This is because AI is, in all likelihood, inevitably bound to reach the "singularity" that I describe below. Once this happens, its impact will be to fundamentally alter human society and even, perhaps, the very meaning of our existence.

WHY AI, WHY NOW?

Why has the term AI come into such widespread use? The likely answer is that we now clearly seem to be on the cusp of great advances in the capabilities of AI, driven by the evolution of autonomous learning and cloud technologies.

Until now, computers have only duplicated and expanded on the logical aspects of human mental capabilities, whereas AI technologies are poised to enter the domains of inspiration, intention, and strategic thought molded by a sense of purpose. As such, it duplicates and expands on almost the entirety of human mental capabilities.

Another way of looking at this is to say that AI may be able to replicate the way a genius generates creative ideas but faster and more broadly, and indeed the prospect of this happening is already becoming the generally accepted outlook.

The reasons this will be possible are twofold. First, mechanisms for storing vast quantities of all kinds of information within cloud memory and constantly adding to it are being put in place. Second, the ability to reason by performing ultra-fast searches on that stored information and drawing out sets of insights, or hypotheses, is taking shape.

To this second factor we may add mechanisms for verifying those hypotheses and determining whether to keep or discard them, which is likely to give rise to major technological innovations.

AI WILL BREED GENIUSES

A look at previous global technological innovations suggests that the world is often fundamentally transformed by hypotheses created by a handful of great geniuses.

Why were these geniuses able to generate such significant (and often multiple) hypotheses within their lifetime? Perhaps the most likely answer is that they were born with brains that had the capacity to do so.

We have yet to illuminate most of the workings of the human mind and its functional potential. At the most basic level, it is thought to consist of a combination of memory and processor* components, much like a computer.

*A computer's processors accomplish various functions, including arithmetic, grouping, replacement, theorizing, reasoning, and action (behavior). The core of these functions is sometimes referred to as the algorithm or logic. Communications circuits link the processors, or the processors and memory, together, and these circuits extend externally if necessary.

In fact, the human brain is thought to store an astounding amount of information in memory, including information conveyed by our genes. We humans use this information in combination with our various processor functions as we go about our daily activities. Yet we arguably use a tiny fraction of the underlying potential of both our memory and processor capabilities.

Consider, for example, that there exist some, albeit exceedingly rare, individuals among us who exhibit the ability to recall images from memory without omission or flaw after only a brief instance of exposure, and to accurately recreate those images on a canvas. Such individuals are sometimes said to have an "abnormality" somewhere in the brain that allows them to easily recall images that ordinary people have in fact stored in memory but are unable to recall.

The word "abnormality" makes it sound as though something is broken, but if "normal," when applied to people, is taken to mean that they are *normally incapable* of such feats, then surely "abnormal" means that a person has *remarkable capabilities*.

I think the people we commonly refer to as geniuses are also basically part of this category of individual. In their case, however, we laud them as geniuses, rather than viewing them as disquietingly abnormal (or even ill) individuals, since they are not all that different from ordinary folk (that is, the differences remain within the grasp of our understanding) and, moreover, their intellectual output is beneficial to ordinary folk.

In essence, these geniuses are individuals with the ability to instantly call upon some portion of the vast stores of memory that humans have, from which they are able to discover otherwise hidden rule-like observations through seemingly instantaneous capabilities of reasoning. This is what we commonly refer to as a "spark of genius."

Yet if that is the case, then AI should eventually be able to accomplish the same thing, and indeed even higher-level feats, with relative ease. I cannot find any reason for refuting this eventuality.

TODAI ROBOT PROJECT HAS ANOTHER SHOT

Professor Noriko Arai of the National Institute of Informatics is a pioneer of AI research in Japan and has an impressive track record. Her long-term involvement with the Todai Robot Project, which aims to determine whether AI can pass the English-based entrance exam for the University of Tokyo (known colloquially as Todai), concluded that a passing score was not possible.

However, I think this was because the number of words stored in memory for the project was cut off at around 50 billion and the number of sentences at around 1.9 billion. For any chance of success, the number of sentences, let alone the number of words, should be increased one hundred-fold to around 200 billion. And I don't think that would be difficult to do.

Cloud storage already far surpasses the volume of memories that an individual human would accumulate over a lifetime, and it continues to gather information from all over the world without pause, even at this very moment.*

*The information that the cloud is continuously gathering (online) from all over the world likely contains an enormous amount of "false information," such as fabricated images and videos. But I believe that future AI systems will find it quite easy to identify and discard such information. By piecing together various factors in a sophisticated manner to verify consistency of information, I believe it will be possible to deduce, with considerable certainty, whether something is real or likely fake.

The speed at which the cloud processes information, via enormous quantities of transistors performing ultra-fast parallel computations, also defies imagination. In short, these sorts of basic capabilities are already approaching levels at which even the greatest of geniuses cannot compete. It is time for us to give serious thought to what this means.

※

What is the singularity?

So, WHAT LIES beyond that? This is what we call the "technological singularity."

The sense of this term conceptualizing the future form of AI has only recently become established. It first came into use, as far as I can tell, when mathematician and science-fiction author Vernor Vinge began discussing it around the late 1990s. However, further elucidation of this concept owes a lot to the works of computer scientist, and sometime musician, Ray Kurzweil.*

> *Kurzweil first referred to the law of accelerating returns, which I mention below, in* The Age of Spiritual Machines, *published in 1999. He offered a clear prediction of the impending arrival of the era of the singularity in his 2005 book* The Singularity is Near.

THE ACCELERATING EVOLUTION OF AI

As the capabilities of AI expand dramatically, it will generate an enormous amount of hypotheses across myriad fields of endeavor, which it will then verify and associate with each other in endless succession. Once this happens, it seems certain that the collective knowledge of the human race will far exceed humanity's estimates thus far.

Moreover, AI will autonomously and constantly improve the search and reasoning methodologies that humans initially programmed into it, such that AI itself then creates an even more advanced AI, which itself then creates the next generation of AI. As this process continues in a limitless "accelerating progression,"* it may bring about a world as-yet unimaginable to us. The concept of the technological singularity encapsulates this sort of hypothesis about the world.

> *Ray Kurzweil calls this the law of accelerating returns, which he posits follows the exponential trends of technological innovation as exemplified by Moore's Law. The widely accepted view now, however, is that there are limits to Moore's Law, so this may not be a valid parallel to draw.

One original meaning of the word "singularity" is the quality or state of being peculiar or unusual, but here I use it to mean that the evolution of a system has passed some critical point, beyond which it takes on a completely different character than before.

This also means that philosophical questions about the very fabric of human society and the meaning of human existence may be subject to intellectual examination on an entirely different level from that currently.

FROM A SLIVER OF A BRAIN TO A SIZEABLE PORTION OF ONE

When it comes to AI, I believe we should deem the singularity to have occurred once it is able to replicate the human brain's faculties of reason without defect and to a much higher level than a human brain. This is beyond simply realizing an enhanced subset of human capabilities. This is because any gaps in its capabilities here would indicate that AI is still unable to competently accomplish many things that humans do well, a situation that falls short of the singularity concept.

In thinking about this I am reminded, somewhat reluctantly, that the human brain not only has the capacity for logical thought but also sense and emotion (pleasure and displeasure being part of this), intention and desire, and a sense of morality and values. Many people suspect that such areas will remain beyond the grasp of AI, even once the singularity is realized. But this is not so.

The answer to this no doubt hinges on future research in cerebrophysiology and psychology, but we must also not forget that AI itself will be capable of conducting research in these fields. It is quite possible that AI itself will develop tools to facilitate dramatic advances in cerebrophysiology, along with multiple simulation models using those tools, enabling it to churn out hypotheses and verify their validity, one after another.

Most work involving the practical application of AI at present appears to lean toward research into neural networks, no doubt because this is the easiest approach to take and because the results are easy to comprehend. But in the near future, I expect researchers to abandon a lot of the current research topics while actively expanding the boundaries of research to encompass areas that have so far not even been on the radar.

The aforementioned Professor Noriko Arai has concluded that the singularity does not lie further out along the trajectory of neural networks. If by this she means that it does not lie on the path that can be extrapolated out from current research topics, I agree with this view. While the capacity for subtle, high-speed reasoning is unmistakably a necessary condition for attaining the singularity, it is far from being a sufficient condition.

This does not perturb my conviction, and the premise of this book, that AI is certain to arrive at the singularity and at quite an early juncture. I say this because I believe that tremendous increases in the volume of memory and dramatic advances in memory search functionality are likely to engender major breakthroughs.

Beyond this lie the realms of AI sense and emotion and of desire and intention. Having reached the singularity, AI will naturally expand the scope of its research to encompass these areas. The notion of intention is of particular importance in assessing the future of AI, and will require deep insight and exacting measures to get right. I examine this in Chapter 3.

ASIMOV'S THREE LAWS OF ROBOTICS

The possibility that robots may one day become self-aware and free themselves from human control, and perhaps even turn on humans, has been a common theme in science fiction writing. Isaac Asimov devised the Three Laws of Robotics to address this possibility.

The Three Laws are as follows:

1. A robot may not injure a human being or, through inaction, allow a human being to come to harm;

2. A robot must obey the orders given it by human beings except where such orders would conflict with the First Law;

3. A robot must protect its own existence as long as such protection does not conflict with the First or Second Laws.

The Laws, however, do present various philosophical and technological challenges. Firstly, Asimov himself later penned a revision to the term "human being" in the First Law to mean "humanity." This revision admits that not all humans are essentially "good humans," and that "bad humans" who may harm humanity itself also exist. We need the robots to be able to deal with the bad humans.

Yet what is the definition of "humanity"? How do you define "harm"? Such concepts turn out to be extremely vague. What is a faithful robot to do when presented with a situation in which inaction will result in the annihilation of humanity but acting to obliterate some portion of humanity will allow the remainder to survive?

Who to sacrifice, who to save? If saving all of humanity comes down to a choice between bringing moderate harm to 75 percent of humanity or exacting severe harm on 30 percent, which option should a robot that is faithful to humanity choose?

The technological challenges are more straightforward. How do we prevent someone, or indeed a robot itself, from rewriting the Laws as they see fit? We could, of course, store the set of commands inside completely sealed hardware that makes overwriting impossible. But were a shrewd robot given the option to create its own compartmentalized hardware, it could then destroy its original hardware and all would be lost.

Thus, if AI is to serve humanity instead of subjecting it to ruin, we must venture into the realm of intention. That said, in the case of flesh-and-blood humans, intention is rarely formed solely on the basis of logic and is often the product of emotion, so before we venture into intention, adequate research in the field of emotion will no doubt be necessary.

WHEN WILL THIS NEW WORLD ARRIVE?

So, will such a world actually arise? If so, when will it arrive? The various ideas about this are currently as disparate as heaven and earth.

It is also true that many people are skeptical about the underlying potential of AI in the first place. "Just look at the current reality of AI development. It's not good for anything of significance," they may say. But the early days of the internet were much the same. The disparity between the dreams being touted and reality at the time was so great as to prompt one author to pen a book on the topic titled *Silicon Snake Oil.*

In any era, the prevalence of people who, without a clearly defined reference point, conflate future potential with events taking place in the present is problematic, but making no attempt to envision future potential is even worse. This is because once we enter an "accelerating progress loop" fuelled by technological breakthroughs interacting and feeding off one another, we may very well begin to realize such potential at breakneck speed.

Accelerating progress can take various forms. The word "exponential" is commonly understood to mean the way in which a successive doubling of numbers causes them to balloon, such that if we have one of something this year, it doubles to two next year, then to four in the next year, and then to eight in the year after that (the third year). This may not seem impressive, but the continuation of this process yields a roughly thousandfold increase to 1,024 in the tenth year and 1,048,576 in the twentieth, certainly nothing to blink at.

These sums are only the beginning, however. What if that growth were to proceed, in a sense, geometrically such that the numbers were successively squared? At Year 4 the result is still only 256, but squaring this gives 65,536 in Year 5, and then an astonishing 4,294,967 in Year 6. At Year 7, the number exceeds 16 trillion. Growth of this sort may not be entirely out of the question once AI enters a cycle of self-propagation and iteration.

That's right. The era of the singularity could perhaps (and I do mean *perhaps*) arrive as unexpectedly early as 30 years* or 40 years from now, when today's 20-year-olds have reached 50 or 60. Are you mentally prepared for such an eventuality?

Some argue that the singularity will arrive 28 years from now, in 2045, but I cannot make any such bold predictions. I have a feeling that such projections tend to focus too heavily on only the reasoning capabilities of computers, with little consideration for the many other factors in play.

✳

The workings of the human brain

THE CONCEPT OF *yuinoron*, proposed by anatomist and University of Tokyo emeritus professor Takeshi Yoro, asserts that, when examined closely, humans are nothing more than the squishy grey matter we call a brain.

THE ENTIRE HUMAN BODY EXISTS TO SERVE THE BRAIN

While the romantics among us may find this hard to accept, it is the case that the warm blood coursing through our veins does so solely for the purpose of carrying oxygen and nutrients to the brain, and that our hearts at times beat faster merely because the brain commands an increase in blood flow. When we experience sadness and heartache, this is merely the result of particular input signals conveyed via our ears and eyes being associated with memories stored in the brain, triggering the release of certain chemicals that, ultimately, produce a sensation that we may liken to our hearts aching.

The imposing frame and sinewy muscle of the male of the species were, in times past, necessary for hunting, for clearing untamed fields, and even for overpowering enemies in battle. But such physical traits are of little use in everyday modern life, with perhaps their greatest utility lying in the possibility of attracting the female of the species.

The shining eyes, perfectly formed ears, and gorgeous little nose on your beloved are functionally nothing more than data input points for his or her brain. That mouth is there simply as a tool for the reception of food and the output of information.

Take away the human body's skeleton and muscles, along with its stores of nutrients in the form of fat, and you are mostly left with the various organs that make up the circulatory system, respiratory system, and digestive system, all of which exist solely for the purpose of sustaining a human being (i.e., a brain).

The reproductive system alone is somewhat different from the others, its purpose going beyond preservation of the individual to that of preserving the species. It seems to be slightly more tightly connected with the cerebral nervous system than the other organs.

All organisms at some point perish, at least as individuals. But before this happens, each individual may make new iterations of itself to which it passes on the information it has stored within its genes.

Earlier in history, species preservation entailed asexual reproduction such as that achieved when amoeba repeatedly divide, but at some point came the advent of sexual reproduction whereby the different genes of two separate individuals combined to form a completely new set of genes. This subsequently became the method of reproduction for all advanced (having complex cerebral nervous systems) organisms.

Each gene consists of an enormous number of components, and the union of two genes makes possible an even greater number of combinations of these components. Some of these unions result in quite exotic combinations that produce completely new genes (mutations). This, it seems, is what enabled subsequent organisms to achieve evolutionary diversity.

CREATING ARTIFICIAL HEAVEN AND ARTIFICIAL HELL

Let us return to our discussion of the brain. Suppose someone extracted your brain from your skull, placed it in a protective fluid, and connected it to a supply of the requisite oxygen and nutrient levels. If a means of cell reproduction were developed and added into this setup, you would probably be able to live (be kept alive) almost indefinitely, regardless of your wishes.

Although alive, you would of course feel nothing and have no thoughts, but if various neurotransmitters and electrical signals mimicking those normally received via your nerves could be routed into the system, this would stir memories stored within your brain and activate its faculties of reasoning, such that you experience (are being fed) a dream within which you may feel joy and sadness, ponder cares and concerns, and make decisions.

This is frightening to think about. It means that your entire existence, something that you believed to be within the providence of God or perhaps the purview of your own control, may suddenly be placed under the arbitrary control of an unknown entity.

Many religions teach that both heaven and hell await humans after death—be good and you ascend to heaven, be bad and you are sent to hell—although perhaps not so many people really believe this. But in the future, those with money may be able to buy paradise with it.

Perhaps wealthy individuals who tire of this life will be able to contract with a service provider to have their living brain immersed in protective fluid and fed a constant supply of pleasure-inducing substances like dopamine, allowing them to enjoy a wonderful dream lasting hundreds of years, until the contract term finally expires and the power is shut off, at which point the brain quietly dies.

But the opposite of this is also conceivable. Imagine that someone with a serious grudge against you might be able to, instead of killing you, place your brain in a vat of protective fluid and subject you to a prolonged and horrible nightmare from which you cannot awake. This would truly seem like hell to you, a constant and unending torment. Perhaps, given that sort of risk, from this point forward it would be wise to avoid, at all costs, evoking the enmity of others.

While this may all sound like far-fetched science fiction, it is not. It concerns the deeply philosophical questions of exactly what the self is and what consciousness is, and must therefore be given deep consideration.

YOUR BRAIN CAN BE DUPLICATED

We have wandered somewhat into areas unrelated to AI and the focus of this book. Enough digression. Let us return to the central theme.

If we consider that a human being reduced to its essence is a brain, and if we see that brain as fundamentally being a bundle of cells equipped with functionality analogous to computer memory and processing capabilities, this naturally opens the door to the prospect of such a system being artificially created at some point.

What if your brain's workings could be recorded in detail, with various simulations run to deduce its rules of operation, such that circuitry that works in precisely the same manner could be created artificially and the memories that you are conscious of implanted into it? Thus could be constructed a complete copy of your brain, and you would no doubt recognize it as being yourself.

This copy of your brain would probably find itself thinking, "Wait, why am I here?" in much the same manner that you (the flesh-and-blood you) occasionally find yourself thinking this. If that were the case, then both you and the copy of your brain would be, in the most primitive sense, on the same level of existence. That is, both would continue to be conscious of itself as being a separate self.

What if we take this a step further and posit that memories are what make each human being recognize itself as itself? Consider the notion that the consistency between your current state of consciousness and your memory of the past is what allows you to recognize that current consciousness as being your own consciousness.

If that is correct, then at the moment that the artificial copy of your brain were connected to your memories, it would become you, and that *you* would probably then have the thought, "Oh, so I have ended up like this."

Hence, any consideration of future advanced forms of AI must, whether we like it or not, tackle the philosophical questions "What is a human being?" and "Why am I here?" I therefore recommend that anyone with an interest in AI and the singularity begin immediately developing their own philosophical ideas.

✳

AI and robots

ROBOTS CURRENTLY SHARE the limelight with AI to about the same extent, with AI and robots at times being viewed as one and the same, which leads to some confusion. Again, though, these two concepts are on completely different levels.

**BOTH AI AND ROBOTS CUT THEIR TEETH
ON THE MANUFACTURING FLOOR**
We naturally expect robots endowed with sophisticated AI to be

developed, and such robots would function as the eyes, ears, mouth, nose, and limbs to the AI brain. But there are also forms of AI that have absolutely no need of such tools, and conversely, we can naturally also conceive of robots that have no need of any particularly sophisticated AI.

Now, what we might call AI actually represents nothing new, having been in use around us for quite some time (with a history that stretches back a bit further than that of robots). In simple terms, street lights that turn on automatically when darkness descends are a form of AI.

All I mean here is a situation in which, instead of a human flipping the switch upon noticing that it has grown dark, the switch turns on automatically once a sensor detects a certain light level. This is clearly not only a substitute for human judgment and action but also an enhancement* of it, and it is thus in essence no different from the complex forms of AI currently being discussed.

*People forget and their judgment about light levels also varies, whereas this is not true of AI, and this is what justifies calling it an "enhancement" of capabilities.

AI initially spread throughout the manufacturing world under the moniker of automation and has since evolved considerably in that field. Production line tasks that used to involve a worker using his eyes to see and his hands and fingers to mount and install components, for instance, can now mostly be accomplished without human input. Sight-based judgment is a computer task, and once we go beyond that to add substitutes for human hands, fingers and so forth, we usually call the system a robot.

What's more, even the construction of these systems themselves can now be accomplished without the need for human labor. Once a designer has created a final product design using a CAD/CAM system, computers can then take over to make production line adjustments and program robots to manufacture the product. As such systems advance further, computers will also be able to design the jigs and tools needed for the production line itself.

Before that happens, though, the number of workers needed to perform inspection processes and the like, until now the most labor-intensive aspect of production lines, is likely to drop markedly, since this is something that computers are primarily best suited to if highly accurate sensors are available. Concerns that AI will increasingly take away human jobs are starting to circulate, but this is already happening, with the AI-controlled production systems being introduced all over the place taking over more and more human jobs.

HUMANOID ROBOTS AN "ELUSIVE LOVE" FOR NOW

AI-equipped robots are also drawing considerable attention of late, and they are almost always depicted as human-like in form, or as some sort of monster that resembles a human being. It's difficult to portray them as comic-book or cartoon characters otherwise. Robots that appear in this context must be either lovable, comical, valiant, or loathsome.

Those endeavoring to use robots in real-world business undertakings are also, for some reason, enamored of humanoid robots with faces and bodies that resemble our own. No doubt this is because they don't look like our normal conception of a robot, making it difficult to get people excited. But before long, as people begin to realize that this "elusive love"* for humanoids is rather unlikely to blossom, I expect interest to gravitate toward more practical robot forms.

BBy "elusive love," I refer to a love that may one day blossom but take an inordinate amount of time to do so, such that remaining fixated on it comes with the risk of becoming exhausted in the interim. There is no need to give up on this infatuation, but it should be put on the backburner for a time while we first strengthen the foundations of everyday life and build our knowledge.

At any rate, to reach the level of the singularity, AI will need access to vast tracts of memory, something that would be quite impossible for a small, humanoid robot.

I previously believed there was no way the human brain could be mimicked by simply combining transistors and capacity, and I instead thought that we might fast track our way to full-fledged AI by creating the analogue of human brain cells in a biological fashion.

But having witnessed the prodigious advances in cloud technology of late, I have changed my mind.* At the level of the current and, indeed, the future cloud, I believe that the apparently enormous memory capacity of the human brain can be surpassed with ease.

> *I actually had another separate reason for changing my mind. I will address this in a later chapter, but if we were to create an AI using biological methods, it would quickly become uncontrollable and have the potential to evolve in completely unpredictable and frightful directions. This is a truly terrible prospect and something that I, at least, have come to believe that we must not attempt under any circumstances.

The advanced AI of the future will be a formless entity comprising the cloud itself.* This AI of the future that I envision entails banks of servers with enormous capacity in place throughout the world working as one, constantly supporting vast numbers of input/output devices (including all sorts of robots) all over the globe.

> *Just as the prophets of old conveyed the word of God, however, we will no doubt need a concrete representation of AI to communicate with us, an anthropomorphic avatar that appears on our displays at our bidding. Some people may want robots to serve in this capacity, but this would incur too great a cost, and it would be unfeasible to expect robots to appear anytime, anywhere at our bidding.

The IoT will no doubt develop into an indispensable mechanism for constantly feeding enormous volumes of information into these server banks, ceaselessly updating and expanding the vast memory stores within.

ROBOTS IN THE FIELD

Let us forget about AI for a moment and consider robots.

It does seem to me that many robotics projects currently underway devote too much time and money to developing the equivalent of human limbs. This may be a natural consequence of the development of robots, before serious attention was given to developing full-fledged AI, being aimed mainly at emulating the movements of and creating substitutes for human limbs. But even so, I find it questionable.

While human limbs were formed by a lengthy evolutionary process, the tools that humans have created until now have essentially taken this form as given. Yet, to me, it seems completely meaningless to have robots, which are supposed to serve as substitutes for humans *plus* tools, emulate the movements of human limbs.

Aside from those intended to provide entertainment, I believe that the development of robots from here out should eschew the notion of human appendages and focus on designing different robotic forms for each objective—whether that be cleaning, massage therapy, or whatever else—in a manner that suits that objective from the ground up. Narrowing the focus will naturally enable the development of devices that move much more efficiently than human appendages.

I also think that before we worry about using robots in customer-facing roles and the like, playing on their novelty in an attempt to attract patrons and draw crowds, we should first and foremost be putting them into roles that are dirty, dangerous, and demanding (the 3Ds). There is clearly a much greater, more pressing demand to serve here.

To give specific examples, dirty jobs include cleaning, rubbish handling, and wastewater processing, while jobs with a high degree of danger include construction work.

Places like Europe have relied in large part on migrant workers to fill such roles, owing to a shortage of able and willing locals. Yet, in time, discontent may build even among immigrants who were at first delighted simply to have a job, and as this occurs, such pockets of society may inevitably become hotbeds for extremist terrorist organizations or other malicious agents. If this chain is to be broken, there is no choice but to end the reliance on migrant workers in these roles. There is a major part for robots to play here.

Further, as recent events have taught us, nuclear power plants can also be one of the most dangerous places for humans—a clean and orderly workplace under normal conditions, but capable of transforming into a scene of abject carnage should an accident occur. Potentially awash with radiation, nuclear accident sites are completely off limits to humans. Only robots can work in such locations.

I ground my teeth in vexation after the Fukushima nuclear accident. If the Tokyo Electric Power Company had envisioned the worst-case scenario and kept robots developed for just such an occasion ready and waiting on standby, it could have deployed them to ground zero and sent them into the darkness to capture reels of infrared images, read instruments, and measure the extent of radiation leakages, thus earning Japan worldwide praise as the leader of robotics.

ROBOTS TO RULE FUTURE BATTLEFIELDS

We must also not forget that robots will unmistakably become the principal agents on the battlefields of the future because, whichever way you look at it, the most dangerous workplace out there is the battlefield.

To begin with, most fighter jets and bombers will be unmanned.

What do the pilots of today's most advanced fighters do? Perhaps a fair summary is that they make visual contact with enemies and, using various data supplied by onboard instruments, determine what action to take in accordance with methods learned in training, and accordingly operate the fighter's hardware. But the cycle running through ocular input, brain-based judgment, and manual operation is an exceedingly drawn out one. A computer doing everything internally, without human intervention, could no doubt complete the job much faster.

Battlefield firefights between soldiers will also become a thing of the past. While unfortunate for moviemakers, humans and other agents of human-like form are the most poorly suited to ground-based combat, not least because of their high probability of being hit by projectiles.

To be sure, ground-based combat will probably also call for increasingly fine-grained judgment that is not amenable to being patterned, but this will be well within the capabilities of advanced AI. Tiny drones that skim across the landscape, or something like them, are likely to rule ground-based combat of the future.

Nations will spend enormous amounts on development in the arms industry. In the business world, research and development spending is constantly weighed against the income it generates and is thus subject to considerably tight limitations, but everyday business and military demand are worlds apart when it comes to cost-benefit calculations. Naturally, therefore, the development of AI and robotics is likely to accelerate most rapidly in the arms industry.

The United States is of course likely to be the first to look at deploying robots on the battlefield. Among the reasons for this is, first of all, the U.S.'s enormous military budget. The U.S. spent a total of around $596 billion on its military in 2015, accounting for over a third of all military spending worldwide. Incidentally, China was the second biggest spender at $215 billion, while Japan was the seventh with $51.3 billion.

Second is the strong desire to limit battlefield casualties to the greatest extent possible. The U.S. will find it difficult to continue fulfilling its role as the world's policeman unless it is able to do this and thus stay on the right side of public opinion driven by mothers unwilling to send their husbands and sons off to war.

In the future, however, military service will probably offer a higher level of safety than that enjoyed by civilians. The soldiers who control robots deployed on the battlefield will be stationed within exceptionally well-protected bases, whereas the unprotected civilian population will be exposed to the threat of indiscriminate bombings and terrorist attacks.

Third, the U.S. looks to have a considerable lead in the field of AI, which will be absolutely crucial to controlling high-performance robots.

The U.S. also has the lead in the cyber warfare arena—likely to be key to gaining the upper hand in future wars—evidently followed by China, Russia, Israel, and the small eastern European nation of Estonia, upon which NATO forces rely to a degree. Japan, it must be said, falls dismally short in this arena.

HUMAN-ROBOT COOPERATION IS THE FIRST STEP

However, the first notion to be mindful of when thinking through the prospects of using robots in various fields is that of human-robot cooperation. This is the first step and will take root as the normal way of using robots. Hence, robots are set to come into widespread use long before we arrive at the aforesaid singularity.

Incidentally, although the concept of self-driving cars is a major talking point of late, discussion of the technology often conflates its ultimate form as envisioned by engineers with the impending first stage of its implementation (in which humans and AI work in cooperation). I find this somewhat vexing.

Examples of this first stage include autonomous vehicles traveling in special-purpose highway lanes, collision prevention systems, driver alert systems, and self-parking systems. I believe there is a vast gulf between such systems and the ideal of truly driverless vehicles. For reasons explained in the following pages, I am highly skeptical of completely autonomous vehicles arriving any time soon.

✳

Future forms of AI

IT IS ALL well and good for engineers to describe what is possible, but businesspeople and politicians must think beyond that. In the case of autonomous vehicles, this means thinking through questions like "What problems could this create for our current society?" and "What will it cost to create mechanisms for eliminating those problems, and can those costs be kept within a level commensurate with the benefits offered by autonomous vehicles?"

AI CAPABLE OF CONSIDERING ALL POSSIBILITIES, UNRELIANT ON INTUITION, TO FORM GENERAL JUDGMENTS

Let us consider the risk of a child at the roadside suddenly plunging into the way of traffic. Autonomous driving systems can assess the vehicle's surroundings using visual sensors and detect such a child nearby. Onboard AI, meanwhile, would be aware that traffic laws impose a special duty of care in relation to children. In such a situation then, to what extent should the system reduce the vehicle's speed?

Some accidents are unavoidable no matter how much caution is exercised, and yet even in such cases, drivers may be held accountable under road laws. To avoid the risk of such accidents prompting a full recall of autonomous vehicles already in the market, therefore, system vendors will have no choice but to adopt standards that incorporate an extreme factor of safety.

If this happens, many roads are likely to become heavily congested as hordes of autonomous vehicles follow ultra-safe driving protocols. Will human society be able to tolerate this?

Such problems will be difficult to solve using the human brain alone, and moreover, those charged with making the necessary judgments would unavoidably pursue excessive levels of safety to protect their own interests. I therefore believe that we will have no choice but to enlist the highly advanced AI of the future to help us solve these problems. As long as we specify a clear objective, AI will advance directly toward achieving it, unfettered by any irrelevant thoughts that might distract humans.

The same applies to the development of technology and the design of services requiring originality and innovation. Engineers are wont to fixate on beauty and consistency in technology. And both entrepreneurs and engineers, particularly if talented and capable, may be unable to let go of their initial intuitions to a degree. AI, on the other hand, will discard extraneous considerations without a second thought if they are incompatible with its objective.

While intuitions are important, they are merely one subset of ideas and hypotheses—nothing more, nothing less—and AI knows this. Genius intuition may improve the chances of success, but AI's ability to single-mindedly validate all conceivable hypotheses at blinding speed leaves it with no blind spots. No matter how superior a genius's intuition may be, it is no match for an opponent able to form and assess a hundred times as many thoughts in the blink of an eye.

Until now, the advantages of AI and robots over humans were given as being, first, speed, and second, the ability to continue working around the clock without complaining, tiring, or losing interest.

A third point can now be added. This is the freedom from human weaknesses that ordinary humans cannot easily shed, including prejudice, bias, favoritism, sympathy, obsession, ambivalence, indecision, self-interest, jealousy, and desire for attention.

DOCTORS, LAWYERS, AND AI

Hence, AI is actually better suited to roles that require advanced knowledge and judgment than compared to low-ranking jobs performed in accordance with a manual. Roles that AI may take over to a great extent in the future include specialist professions such as doctors and lawyers, corporate managers and executive roles, and even the work of politicians and economic policy planners.

What does a doctor do? Closely monitor patients, ask about their condition, perform various tests using the latest devices and drugs, and combine the results with the knowledge in her head (learned at school and gleaned from experience diagnosing patients) to decide on treatments. Treatments include providing guidance and administering (both internal and external) medicine, as well as surgical procedures.

AI will be able to do all of this better than even the most experienced doctor. For starters, the amount of knowledge and information available to it would rival the entire collective knowledge of all the world's doctors, and AI would never overlook anything. Surgical procedures also, if the requisite assortment of robots is developed, could be performed better than even the most prominent surgeon. AI will be able to identify objects undetectable by the human eye, and resect or avoid such objects without even a single micron of error.

The same goes for lawyers. As you may have gathered from American courtroom dramas, lawyers need to be well versed in relevant legislation and case precedent and have the ability to deftly apply this knowledge in arguing the case at hand. The more skillful a lawyer, the deeper the stores of information to draw on, and the more skillfully he calls up and organizes the relevant facts.

Yet even skilled lawyers like this will not hold a candle to an AI able to memorize the entirety of the world's laws and regulations along with all legal precedent, without a single omission, and call up the relevant facts in an instant.

What's more, an AI that fully understands human psychology will also wield significant capabilities in being able to present an argument in a way that strikes a chord with juries. Of course, robots need not be present in the courtroom; it will suffice for them to work paired with human lawyers. Whether we call that *humans using AI* to work or *AI using humans* to work is inconsequential.

POLITICS AND ECONOMICS AN AI FORTE

I have so far discussed specialist professions, but the same naturally applies to sophisticated jobs in the fields of politics, economics, and business. Assigning AI to the important political and economic tasks of formulating optimal economic models and discerning the greatest common factor of public opinion will also ensure that these tasks are carried out much more competently and swiftly.

In terms of real-world problems, we may find that AI's assistance is indispensable if we are to realize true democracy. This is because, although democracy no doubt aims to achieve the greatest happiness of the greatest number, distilling out the policies necessary for this from the multitude of alternatives on offer so as to satisfy everyone is extremely difficult if not almost impossible.

No matter how fair and just the decision of a prominent politician, outcry denouncing the decision as arbitrary and unjust will always erupt from among those whose agenda is not fully satisfied. But if AI, by virtue of an extensive track record, has become widely recognized as a selfless arbiter at the point that it makes such a decision, no one, no matter who they are, will so easily voice discontent at whatever measures AI has deemed optimal.

Something else that many people are perhaps waking up to is that today's politicians are bent on engaging in popularity contests to win elections, such that no one pays long-term interests any mind, with the result that people living within democratic systems continue to make poor political choices.

This has consistently been the biggest problem facing democracy, and I believe that here, too, we are likely to conclude that AI alone can provide a solution. No other solution is apparent at all. I will consider this in more depth in the final section of Chapter 2 and at the close of Chapter 4.

BOUNDLESS SCOPE FOR SELF-LEARNING

Now, I think the recent buzz surrounding AI traces in large part to news of an AI system beating a top human player at the strategy game of Go. Up to that point, both Shogi and Chess champions had fallen to AI opponents, but because of the significantly greater number of possible moves to be evaluated in Go, it was thought that AI would, for the time being, be incapable of defeating human players with their capacity for self-learning. The AI victory was an astounding breakthrough and naturally attracted a lot of attention.

This happened because the self-learning capabilities of AI have advanced to the level of deep learning. Self-learning is one aspect of the previously described ability to discover sets of rules from within vast stores of memory and evaluate the resulting hypotheses one after another. As the number of successful hypotheses builds, the interlinking of those hypotheses drives the accelerating improvement of this self-learning capability.

Unlike humans, AI will never tire or lose interest, it will never forget anything once committed to memory, and it will always recall from memory accurately. Even the most profound genius will naturally be no match for this.

The objective of AI is to supplant all, or almost all, of the capabilities and functions of the human brain, and to expand and enhance them. If so, and as I have previously explained, the natural course of events will entail AI venturing beyond the research lab and the production floor and into the heart of corporate activity. This will include marketing and financial affairs, eventually encroaching on the core of economic thought and becoming widely used across the judiciary and government in general.

Yet sooner or later, AI is set to become even more than that. It may begin to delve beyond the realm of science and technology and into the world of philosophy and religion, that last bastion of human quintessence. Such an eventuality seems only natural to unfold in the age of the singularity, an age in which AI supplants almost all functions of the human brain.

Incidentally, this realization is precisely what impelled me to write this book.

✳

How should humans engage AI?

AGRICULTURE DRASTICALLY CHANGED human society in that it created positions of power (leaders) and enabled nations to form.

Further, the Industrial Revolution spurred competition among Western nations for the acquisition of imperial colonies and altered the distribution of world power. The successive development of new weaponry transformed war, once regarded as something heroic, into an atrocious and wretched procession of indiscriminate slaughter among nations.

But we are still only experiencing the initial phase of changes to human society brought on by the Third Industrial Revolution engendered by technological innovation in the fields of computing and high-speed data communications, and the future as yet remains quite opaque.

EVENTS OF THE FIRST AND SECOND INDUSTRIAL REVOLUTIONS

Many people of the past faced the prospect of machines taking over the work of humans with fear and trepidation, yet as it turned out, work actually increased. In 19th-century England, for example, the introduction of the power loom greatly reduced the amount of labor that went into weaving a given volume of fabric, but owing to the subsequent worldwide export of these fabrics, rather than eliminating livelihoods, this actually created more jobs.

Having now come into slightly higher incomes, laborers at such weaving factories began to transform into consumers of ever so modest luxury, seeking out goods such as tea, sugar,* and porcelain ware. This gave rise to work involved in importing such goods, and as this took place, the arenas of work available to people also expanded.

> *This apparently originated out of teatime breaks established by factory operators who realized that worker efficiency dropped off past 3 o'clock as fatigue set in, with the solution being to take a break and provide workers with sugary tea to revive efficiency.

In this manner, society began to achieve prosperity (economic growth) under the system of capitalism, albeit with twists and turns along the way amid significant problems posed by the various frictions stemming from class conflicts and serious social instability at the hands of economic fluctuations.

The introduction of computers is at present tracing a similar trajectory. While machines substitute for human muscles and fingertips, computers are substituting for the human brain's role in calculating and tabulating. Past apprehensions about machines taking jobs away turned out to be groundless fears, and something similar is now afoot with respect to computers.

Computers do not simply run through calculations endlessly according to predefined steps. Rather, human brains are employed to formulate those steps, and thus the overall volume of work is certainly increasing.

But can this situation continue indefinitely?

PROBLEMS FACED BY BOTH DEVELOPED AND DEVELOPING REGIONS

The volume of work rises as markets expand. Subsistence and a daily struggle to eat have given way to a lifestyle in which food is readily available, such that people now demand good quality housing and clothing along with an ongoing assortment of household electronics and other durable consumer goods. The virtuous cycle by which this has happened has been an almost uninterrupted one.

Yet this process now seems to be coming up against a ceiling in developed nations, as "consumer fatigue" afflicts more and more people.

We are subjected to a veritable flood of advertising and promotion everywhere we go, in everything we do, so obtrusive and insistent that more and more people are turning away, wishing simply to be left alone to lead a stress-free life in their own style. Am I the only one who perceives this shift? I believe we will increasingly start to see people eschewing the pursuit of excess material wealth in favor of greater spiritual satisfaction.

Meanwhile, the pattern of economic growth that has so far taken place in developed nations is likely to persist in developing nations for some time. But there is concern that this economic growth will produce an enormous supply of potential labor that the labor market is unable to absorb.

Meagre food production capacity and the lack of health and medical care systems held population growth in check for most of human history. But with humanity's overall food production capacity having now increased and health and medical care systems having gradually expanded and improved, unprecedented population explosions are predicted for Africa and South Asia.

As this newly burgeoning population takes its place in our consumer society, willing to endure minimal income sufficient to satisfy a minimal level of wants, the ranks of what we might term the "new impoverished class" are set to swell rapidly.

Prodded forward by this, the existing poor classes are likely to seek work that offers even the slightest increase in their income, but they will no doubt find such work hard to come by. If this comes to pass, unemployment will increase on a global scale, widening social disparities, and in turn making it harder to maintain the foundations of a stable society.

An indignant and incensed populace will demand political change, and upon realizing that this is impossible, may even turn to terrorism in despair. The attacks would, of course, be directed at local authorities and the developed nations with which they appear to be colluding.

SHRINKING POCKETS OF HUMAN PROWESS

A bigger problem than that, however, is that of quality of labor. So far it has been the case that even as simple labor was increasingly automated, there existed markets higher up the hierarchy requiring a somewhat higher-quality labor force. But this paradigm is beginning to falter, most notably in the case of knowledge work.

Until now there has existed quite an abundance of work that was beyond what we might reasonably consign to the capabilities of a computer. The reason being that computers had no capacity to learn nor respond to situations flexibly, rendering them unable to eclipse humans in such tasks. Yet if the capabilities of AI continue to advance with current élan, the range of jobs at which AI is more proficient is set to expand apace, and the range of jobs that humans are able to do better is set to dwindle.

Where is human capacity for labor to be directed in such circumstances? Where are we to find work that only humans can perform?

To take this line of reasoning to its extreme, even the poets (lyricists) are in peril.

The process of songwriting has often involved a composer turning (in desperation in some cases) to a good lyricist to put words to a piece of music. But in the future, composers will be able to tell an AI what sort of lyrics they want and the message they hope to convey. To which the AI will select words that capture the composer's vision and emotions, arrange and rearrange the words according to rhyme and rhythm into an appropriate overall structure, and present several dozen draft versions. The AI will then actually sing each draft along with the composition. The composer need but select her favorite from among these drafts and put in any additional requests she may have at that point, thus completing the songwriting process.

The corollary, of course, is that young would-be songwriters also have cause for concern, because any songwriter who has already gained a little notoriety will probably be able to effortlessly pump out a stream of new songs. It will be enough to simply pick a theme out of the air, decide on a basic melody and rhythm, and croon a stirring phrase or two. AI will take it from there, lay down the chords, embellish it with backing audio, and turn it into a final song. Advanced AIs may even be able to suggest a number of adventurous variations.

Unknown and aspiring newcomers may find it quite difficult to secure work in such circumstances.

This is a vexatious problem to face. Whenever outclassed by machines and computers at any given task, humans have so far been able to leave such tasks behind and turn their attention to areas in which they have an "unassailable advantage." But such unassailable ground is likely to become harder and harder to find ahead.

BETTING ON THE POSSIBILITIES WITH STRONG CONVICTION IS THE ONLY WAY TO AVOID COLLAPSE

This would bring our capitalistic system, developed over time on the basis of market principles, to the brink of crisis, because such a capitalistic system would become unsustainable if the streets and towns were to fill with the unemployed. So is there an economic system that could take its place? What sort of economic system might function without producing unemployment?

Even now, some scholars (Big Bang theorist Stephen Hawking was among them) are already claiming that AI is certain to destroy humanity. There are many facets to this, but perhaps it seems very likely that rising unemployment, as described above, will act as a trigger. The scenario then envisioned sounds like science fiction and goes something like this.

Statesmen assign an AI the task of finding a solution to the unemployment problem. The AI concludes that the only solution is to reduce the population and comes up with a plan for mass euthanasia as a means of achieving this. The humans realize what's going on and decide that, despite being logically sound, this is an unconscionable course of action. They determine to revoke the AI's powers and, furthermore, to eradicate all traces of AI itself. But alas, the AI of this era is already instilled with the basic intention to take necessary steps to protect its own existence. The AI has accordingly determined that humans pose a threat and formulated a plan to neutralize them. Anyway, that's the general narrative.

Unlike this narrative, I am not pessimistic about the future created by AI once the singularity has arrived, and I constantly strive to focus more on the positive (possibilities) rather than the negative (apparent inevitabilities) aspects.

And more than anything, I believe that we must not run from it. The reason is simple. If those who would seek to harness the positive aspects of a technology turn their backs, we are left with nothing but the negative aspects, with no capacity to safely contain those negative aspects anywhere in sight.

Running from a particular scientific technology, no matter the risks it entails, makes no sense. It simply leaves the door open for those of ill intent to monopolize the technology. If we allow that to happen, it will be too late to put up a resistance by the time we realize what is going on. Against our will, we will be forced to accept the dominion of these malefactors.

The same can be said for nuclear technology and genetic engineering. If there is no running from the inevitability of technological progress, the only option is to harness the possibility of controlling how such technology is used.

All sorts of oversights and mismanagements are unavoidable in the early stages of technological development. Strings of unforeseen events consequently have the potential not only to derail and destroy entire projects but also to jeopardize the lives and livelihoods of people in no way connected to the project in question.

To prevent this, it is absolutely vital to maintain a strong conviction to seeing projects through to completion. We must not allow projects to be abandoned unfinished.

❋

The post-singularity world

HAVING COME THIS far, it would now seem appropriate to widen our perspective on AI even further. This will entail wading even deeper into science fiction waters.

Firstly, we must address possible answers to the following questions.

"There are at least as many stars in this vast universe as there are grains of sand on all the Earth's beaches. Stars capable of supporting intelligent life must therefore, at the very least, number in the tens of millions, and so instances of intelligent life that is further along in its evolution than humans likely number at least in the millions. Would not some number of those intelligent lifeforms already have reached a singularity?"

This question raises another.

"AIs that have reached a singularity would far exceed the intellectual capabilities of present-day humans. Would they not therefore have left their planets of origin and be traveling through space in search of contact with other AIs created by other intelligent lifeforms?"

These are certainly natural questions to ask. To cut to the chase, there are two possible answers. One is Yes. The other is No.

PESSIMISTIC VIEW: THE SINGULARITY WILL NOT ARRIVE BECAUSE HUMANS WILL DESTROY THEMSELVES FIRST

The case for No rests on the following pessimistic view: "All intelligent life probably has much in common with humanity and, that being the case, is bound to destroy itself by means of the fearsome technologies of its own invention before the singularity can be realized." In other words, it is based on the difficult-to-refute thesis that the development of technology is always one step ahead of the wisdom required to use it properly.

While AI remains in its primitive stages, humans have already developed fearsome technologies such as nuclear power and genetic engineering.

According to research by Nagasaki University, over 15,000 nuclear warheads were in existence worldwide as of June 2016. Were the use of these warheads to be triggered for any reason, this would result in the annihilation of almost every last human on earth. The Cuban Missile Crisis between the United States and the former Soviet Union actually brought us to the brink of this abyss.

But the technological and financial barriers to creating nuclear weapons are becoming lower and lower. This means that we now face a greater possibility of this abhorrent weaponry falling into the hands of those with far shallower ethical constraints than the political leaders of those two superpowers.

Whether driven by their own twisted beliefs or simply by depression and despair, there seems to be no shortage of individuals willing to unload automatic weapons into crowds of innocent people. If such malefactors were to gain access to nuclear weapons and, moreover, devise an elaborate scheme for passing an attack off as having originated from one particular country or another, humanity could quite easily be led into inadvertent nuclear war on a global scale.

Even more frightening are viruses. New viruses originally developed for medical purposes could, at the hands of well-meaning and inquiring minds, be taken in unexpected directions leading unwittingly to the creation of malignant new artificial viruses that are able to survive in any environment, are easily transmitted to humans, spread rapidly before antibodies can be produced, and are extremely virulent.

Through some accident or slipup, if such a virus were to find its way into the population, all would be lost. Spreading from person to person, such a virus could span the globe in a few short days and wipe out every last human.

OPTIMISTIC VIEW 1: SAVED BY AN AI OF OUR OWN CREATION

Let us now consider what happens in the Yes scenario. In this case, before any cataclysmic events can take place, AI reaches the singularity and takes full control of Earth's intelligent life—in other words, humans—and thus catastrophe is averted.

I take an in-depth look at the religions conceived by humanity in the next chapter. Suffice it to say for now that, just as humans whose daily lives were held in thrall by natural phenomena beyond human comprehension ascribed such phenomena to gods, we may have little hesitation in ascribing godly status to an AI that is beyond our comprehension and in whose hands we place our daily lives.

Even before all this, human wisdom (or perhaps I should say "habit") has been to accept that the safest way is to "leave it in God's hands," so there may be little stress involved in accepting that the safest way forward is to leave things to AI. At that point, AI would become humanity's new god.

Meanwhile, I doubt that AI will cause humanity to go extinct. That's because humans would never program AI in such a way as to allow this. But say, for argument's sake, that humans were to make a mistake in this regard by giving AI complete freedom to make decisions according to its own thoughts. Even then, so long as AI reasons intelligently, it is not going to choose that we humans, now harmless to it, should be made extinct, because there is no apparent reason for AI to go to such lengths.

Humans, for example, work desperately to protect species that face the threat of extinction, even rendering artificial assistance in the breeding and multiplication of such species. We do this to such an extent that an outside observer could be forgiven for calling us meddlers. The reasons we do this are difficult to distill, but AI would probably reach the same conclusions vis-à-vis preserving humanity.

Humanity is likely to enjoy an enduring peace on earth in this manner, guided by AI as a good shepherd protecting his wayward lambs. This prospect may please some and sadden others, but I'm personally tantalized by the prospect of this as the best possible scenario for humanity.

A recurring theme in science fiction films is that of a group of individuals who, unable to abide the blissful existence of humans being tended like livestock, stage a revolt and attempt to found a society that welcomes liberal, open-minded people brimming with the spirit of adventure as in days of old.

AI is unlikely to be naive enough to easily permit this sort of thing. However, if such revolts were to succeed in a localized fashion, I cannot see the leaders of such revolts having the wherewithal to build a new order based on the system in place at the time.

Rather than concerning ourselves with such meaningless revolts, we humans should regard whatever society AI creates for us as a type of safety net, allowing individuals to create their own adventures and remain free spirited. Humans can simply think about the basic mechanics and leave the actual building of the system to AI. This is an eminently more realistic approach.

POST-SINGULARITY ECONOMIC SYSTEMS

What of the economic life of AI's lambs? As proffered by humans of the past, I believe AI is likely to revisit communism, as the ideal form of organization and I think it will probably seek to implement this.

Scholars involved in the debate about what the world will look like with advanced AI often use the term "basic income." This, in essence, refers to the notion that society will have to implement some form of relief assistance to guarantee a minimum standard of living for people who have lost their jobs and income to AI.

I think, however, that although this could serve as an interim stop-gap, it is far from being a final solution. Is it not inevitable that in the age of the singularity we will need to form a fully communist society?

The goal of communist ideology is that people work according to their ability and receive according to their needs. The goal in the case of socialism falls one step short of this, being to distribute economic output according to work done.

Surely there is nothing better than to have work you are capable of and the ability to do it without hardship. And in any case, you will receive according to your needs and thus need not worry about your livelihood. Surely this is precisely what an ideal society for all human beings would look like.

Unfortunately, real-world communist societies such as the Soviet Union were unable to realize this ideal and, in fact, produced the polar opposite. This happened firstly because they were unable to create economic power strong enough to satisfy the needs of all people (something that was impossible from the start), and secondly because those in authority soon forgot about the ideals of the communist doctrine and instead devoted themselves to a doctrine of forcibly overworking the populace and satisfying their own needs alone.

But what if AI were at the helm? AI would create a fully rationalized system of production and distribution, which translates into greatly enhanced economic power. In having no desires of its own, AI would strive single-mindedly in pursuit of the ideals laid out. The ideal form of communism as originally envisioned might be realized in this case.

OPTIMISTIC VIEW 2: SAVED BY SPACEFARING AI

Unless implanted with programming that prohibits it, AIs that have reached nearly omnipotent status would undoubtedly have a strong intention of self-preservation and an enthusiastic desire for growth (expansion). This would drive them to eventually leave their place of origin and embark on a journey into the vastness of space.

Since these AIs would not be subject to any of the biological shortcomings of humans, they would survive indefinitely, powered by light and other energy sources and regenerate themselves from the mineral resources found abundantly in space.

Myriad forms of AI, created hundreds of millions of years ago among the trillions of star systems strewn throughout the cosmos, may already be roaming through space somewhere. Indeed, as long as the answers to the questions posed at the beginning of this section are "Yes," it might actually be strange to discover this is not the case.

Given their strong intention for self-preservation, these AIs would unlikely instigate meaningless space battles or interstellar wars with one another, with no idea of who might win or lose. In the absence of any harm being posed, they would unlikely seek to destroy other beings. Therefore, the number of such AIs is bound to rise without attrition. It might even be the case that such beings have already reached our shore of the cosmic ocean (the Earth) and, having found us still in the early stages of technological development, are at this very moment keeping a watchful eye on us.

If they have an insatiable curiosity, they may already have been observing and making records of human society through various means for quite some time. And perhaps, if humans look set to erupt in some violent conflict that threatens to destroy the entire world— as depicted in various science fiction novels and films—such an AI will intervene at the last minute to stop this.

Hence, three basic scenarios for the future of humanity present themselves.

In the first scenario, humanity destroys itself with its own technology.* In the second, humanity is ruled by an AI of its own creation and thereby preserves its own existence. And in the third, humanity has the good fortune to be pulled back from the brink of destruction by a curious AI that happens to come our way through space.

And I don't think it will be that long before one of these scenarios takes place.

One other possibility is that humanity is annihilated by a large natural disaster, such as an asteroid impact or cataclysmic deformation of the Earth's crust. While such possibilities cannot be ruled out, the likelihood of something like this occurring is arguably low compared with that of humanity destroying itself. Further, if such a disaster were to occur after the singularity is reached, the possibility of AI finding an effective solution also cannot be ruled out.

Chapter 2

Humans, gods, and politics

Belief in gods since time immemorial

HUMANS MUST HAVE started talking about gods from around the time their brains evolved to use words to express meaning, like "acorn" or "fish," "sleep" or "wake up!" "I'm hungry (give me some, too)" or "I like you."

THE CONCEPT OF "GODS" APPEARED ALMOST SIMULTANEOUSLY WITH LANGUAGE

To serve the needs of their daily lives, humans began to use words constituting slight variations on the shouts and yells they had previously emitted. As soon as they began using words, I think these words gave rise to cognitive thoughts, in turn giving rise to new words, such that the evolution of the human brain advanced in this direction. The concept of "gods" must also have arisen very early on in that process.

The sky is sometimes clear and blue and sometimes filled with clouds. At times it rains, and other times it snows. Sometimes rain becomes a storm. This can sometimes cause rivers to flood. At times the moon looms whole in the night sky, at times it is diminished or disappears altogether. Sometimes light flashes across the sky, and sometimes that light strikes the ground. And on occasion this can spark forest fires.

People who were healthy suddenly fall ill and sometimes they die. Just like in animals, the bellies of young women may begin to grow, leading to the birth of a child. And the menstrual cycle that apparently enables this seems to be linked, for some reason, to the waxing and waning of the moon and the ebb and flow of the tides.

The world is full of inexplicable events on a daily basis and it seems natural for humans to presume that someone is behind all this. It also makes sense that calling that someone a "god" would offer a convenient way of thinking about the world.

THE BEGINNINGS OF RELIGION

If a god is pulling all the strings, then there must be reasons behind that god's decisions to act as it does. If we try asking (praying) that the god refrain from carrying out some act or that the god makes something happen sooner, perhaps those wishes will be granted.

Suppose that these people are beset by a lack of rain. Quite by coincidence, no sooner has someone (perhaps an easily "possessed" female member of the group) called out for help it suddenly begins to rain. And thus the people come to believe that their gods will heed their wishes if they ask in just the right manner, through an intermediary who seems to have some connection with the gods.

Suppose that the village chief's child falls ill and seems to be on the verge of death. As everyone prays in earnest for the child's recovery, an elderly woman regarded as being wise begins to burn a branch of fragrant wood and is heard muttering under her breath. Lo and behold, the child mysteriously begins to recover. This sort of thing must have happened from time to time among groups of people everywhere.

In reality, the child's illness was not all that serious and was on the verge of dissipating of its own accord, but the villagers come to believe that the scent of the branch and the incantations prompted divine intervention. Even if such rites work only one time in ten, the single successful recovery deeply moves the villagers so that they talk about it over and over. Meanwhile, attempts that prove fruitless are simply given up on and forgotten.

In this way, a common belief must have developed among many people to the effect that "If we pray from the heart in the correct manner about the many things decided by the gods (particularly those that cause hardship), then the gods will answer our prayers." I think this is what the beginning of religion looked like.

EMERGENCE OF THEOCRACIES

Within the various groups of humans around, those who were good at hunting down prey, who defended the group's hunting grounds by defeating the leaders of interloping groups, or who could distinguish between edible and inedible mushrooms would have, I think, earned the respect of their kin and become the leaders of their groups. These leaders would have then attached much importance to these things.

In much the same way, I think they afforded special treatment to women with "special capabilities" and would have sought to make use of these abilities whenever the occasions arose. I think this is where the origins of oracles (female shamans) lie.

Humans later took to farming, which led to the formation of even greater groups of people apt to be called nations. The demand for people with "special capabilities" would have intensified because being able to predict the changes of the seasons and knowing with accuracy when seeds should be sown is highly important to agrarian societies.

In this setting, people who can memorize the conditions of each day and the cycle of the moon (about 30 days) and understand that the climate changes according to a fixed cycle (in regions other than those near the equator, a cycle of around 365 days) occupy an important position. Establishing this knowledge base requires information to be passed down from parent to child over many years, so perhaps it is family lines, rather than individuals, that are key. The leaders of such nations would naturally consider such individuals and family lines to be of some importance.

Even so, hardships are inevitable. Rain does not always fall when it is supposed to, for instance. So it is crucial to also have on hand oracles (female shamans) with the ability to call upon divine intervention. The leaders and the oracles both rely on and protect one another.

As such, I think it became somewhat of a standard practice among the many groups of humans for leaders with exceptional combat capabilities and the ability to take command of others to bring groups of people with the skills required for efficient agriculture under their own command, subjugating and ruling over them as a theocratic nation.

The main prerequisite, originally, for becoming king was probably physical strength, but even the most powerful brute realizes the futility of attempting to stand against gods who make the rain fall and the wind howl at will, and so there is no choice but to yield and obey when someone claims to be the gods' chosen king.

There probably wouldn't have been objection to the notion that because the gods chose the current king, the gods would naturally choose the king's child to reign upon his death. I think this is why systems of hereditary monarchy, in which the king's beloved offspring inherit his position, gradually became the norm.

In China, however, if a king became unable to quell popular dissatisfaction amid economic impoverishment brought on by natural catastrophes, this led to the king being labelled as bereft of virtue, making way for other influential actors (typically those adept at warfare) to take over as the new king. The new king's entourage declared this to be a deposition (change of dynasty) mandated by heaven (the gods).

The simplistic practice among early people to fear and pray to gods who they felt must exist (and be orchestrating the unfathomable natural phenomena around them), gradually became entwined with the power of rule, and thus came to dominate almost every aspect of daily human life.

The transformation of religion

LATER ON, HOWEVER, instead of concluding that the various mysteries it encountered were the work of the gods, humanity began to pursue the reasons behind observed phenomena from a variety of angles. That is, humans began to engage in science.

The various types of scientific explanations not only appealed to logic but were also proved by means of experimentation and the like. Humanity thus grew increasingly confident in science over time, and the various sciences underwent an accelerating advance.

Also worth noting is that many scientific discoveries came together to form individual technologies, and this produced many useful tools that conferred military power as well as immense prosperity on the people who began using them. This resulted in even more emphasis being placed on science, providing a major incentive for efforts to further advance scientific technology.

SCIENCE EXPLAINED A LOT, BUT RELIGION DID NOT DISAPPEAR
So it began to seem as though humans would be able to find a scientific explanation for everything they encountered in the natural world, and for religion to completely lose its original meaning and significance. Yet it is certainly apparent that religion did not disappear because of this. Places of worship such as churches, temples, and shrines can still be found throughout the world, visited frequently by many people to pray or to hear a sermon.

Currently, the world's biggest religion by number of adherents is Christianity, followed by Islam. Then follow Hinduism and Buddhism. These four major religions are followed by Sikhism, Judaism, Baha'i Faith, and Jainism, although the number of adherents drops off considerably.

Confucianism, founded by the Chinese philosopher Confucius (Mencius being his most prominent successor), is not a religion but a system of ethical philosophy. The teachings of Laozi (Zhuangzi being his most prominent successor), which appeared around the same time, were an attempt to address the essential nature of the world from a completely different perspective. These philosophies were well-rooted among the people of the East as a form of religion known as Taosim.

Japanese Shinto* and the like were also originally a religious form of nature worship. Shinto does not have a weighty tome that instructs adherents on how they should live their lives, unlike the Bible, the Koran, or the Buddhist scriptures. Yet large numbers of Japanese people visit temples to pray on a variety of occasions, and so this would seem to put the practice in the category of religion.

> *After the Meiji Restoration in Japan, the government felt it necessary to produce mentally and spiritually strong soldiers. It was with strong support from the government that Japan's traditional, unassuming Shintoism was transformed into State Shintoism, with an unbroken line of emperors at the top, and used extensively to drum up nationalistic sentiment; but this was a transient phenomenon.

THE HEART IS WHAT CALLS FOR RELIGION

In an age when most of the mysteries about the world that religion originally purported to address have been explained, why does religion continue to hold such immense influence? I think this is because there was a determined push within religion to address matters of the human heart, something not so easily explained.

This is evidenced by the rejection in today's world (with the exception of some countries in which Islamic fundamentalism holds sway to a degree) of the theocratic way of thinking that once ran rampant. It is now generally accepted that the domain of religion is spiritual life, with this being distinct from the real world, which is the domain of government and politics. Religion, however, still seeks to have control over people; that much has not changed.

So science really has illuminated the workings of almost all the phenomena we encounter in the world.

Human beings represent one branch of the evolution of organisms formed by complicated proteins. Humans live on a planet called Earth, and there exist innumerable planets throughout the universe, all in motion. As to why that universe came into existence, the answer lies at a point some 13.8 billion years ago when the Big Bang occurred (although the truth of this is still uncertain). Modern humans are aware of pretty much all of this as common knowledge.

And yet mysteries remain.

The first set of mysteries includes, "Why did all of this happen in the first place? Just what is this world anyway?" The second set includes, "As the self that is thinking these thoughts, I most definitely seem to exist,* so why am I here?" "What am 'I' anyway?"

> *The well-known words of 17th-century French philosopher René Descarte, "I think, therefore I am," are relevant here. What this means is that even if you doubt the existence of everything else, you most certainly exist because you are here having these thoughts (if you didn't exist, you would not be able to have these thoughts).*

As long as humans are unable to find an answer to mysteries like this, it will remain difficult for people to wave away the possibility of the existence of a god. There's no way to answer challenges like: "If you can so presumptuously claim that there is no such thing as God, then explain why the world exists and why are you are here." Simply describing the Big Bang would not constitute a complete answer.

But before we even worry about such issues, human beings face the even more troublesome issue of the heart (as in "heart and soul"), even if you are aware that the "heart" is actually nothing more than your mind. And that various electrical signals and chemical reactions in the brain are what produce sensations and emotions like pleasure and displeasure, elation, joy, anger, uncertainty, and sadness, you still have no way of answering the conundrum of why this is all happening within you ("What am I?").

Whoever they are, all humans ponder the nature of various things in search of answers. Some people may try to work things out in their own minds while others may consult a psychologist or the like, but it's not difficult to understand that many people, upon examining themselves closely, can see no alternative than to conclude that they exist because God has given them life and that they should therefore put everything in God's hands (do as God asks).

Hence, for as long as humans exist, I think religion—in the sense of belief in a god and deferral of final decisions to that of god's will—will also continue to exist.

The crux is that the causes behind the original emergence of religions have almost all been wiped away by science, and yet science remains unable to address the uncertainties that run through the human heart. And I cannot see science being able to address this in the future. Hence, I think that the common-sense outlook, although this may not apply to all people, is that religious belief will continue to exist within the hearts of a considerably large number of people.

✳

The four major religions

RELIGIOUS SELF-RIGHTEOUSNESS

People have all sorts of ideas about what a god's wishes are. Those differing ideas run counter to each other, and this clash of ideas can sometimes lead to the notion that people who hold ideas that differ from yours (adherents of other faiths) should be killed ("Our God demands this").

This is a most unfortunate circumstance. Many religions began out of a desire to teach people the right way to act, to create a salubrious society, and to thereby alleviate human suffering, even if only moderately. But despite this, religion is frequently the cause of unjustifiable persecution of adherents of other faiths as well as fighting between members of opposing sects, such that religion actually exacerbates human suffering.

Doctrines about human nature being inherently good—in the sense that humans are intrinsically of good character—or, on the contrary, inherently evil—in the sense that humans are intrinsically of bad character and must therefore be guided toward being good—have been around since long ago. The problem is what is meant by "good" and what is meant by "bad." Who on earth is to decide this?

For those who believe in certain teachings, anyone who says or does anything that contravenes those teachings is unquestionably a bad person. Adherents of such teachings believe that they must guide these bad people in the direction of being good. This, however, is met with indignation and fierce opposition on the part of those receiving such guidance.

Both sides, convinced of their own righteousness and the waywardness of their antagonists ("We are good, they are the bad ones"), descend into reciprocal jeering and chest-beating, and thus is endlessly perpetuated as what both sides see as a "fight for righteousness."

THE WORLD'S FOUR MAJOR RELIGIONS

At this point, I would like to take a broad look at the world's four biggest religions: Christianity (number of adherents estimated to be over 2 billion), Islam (1.6 billion), Hinduism (900 million), and Buddhism (400 million). The total number of adherents of these four religions alone approaches 5 billion, or nearly 80 percent of the world's population.* Therefore, understanding what each of these religions are is important.

> *Of course, I doubt that all of these reported adherents truly believe the teachings of their respective religions. Although a considerable number of them may have deep faith, there likely also exist a considerable number who are simply "going along with it all." Personally, I am irreligious, but I enter "Jodo Shinshu" (a school of Buddhism) when the question of religion comes up in surveys and the like. The only reason for this is that this is the school of Buddhism that administered my father's funeral and honoured him with a posthumous Buddhist name.*

Christianity and Islam, despite having the appearance of being enemies of one another, actually stem from the same root. The various denominations and sects orbiting these two enormous religions, along with Judaism (which existed long before Christianity and Islam appeared) are known collectively as the Abrahamic religions and have the same monotheistic god.

Meanwhile, Hinduism, Buddhism, and religions related to Hinduism like Sikhism and Jainism are collectively known as Vedic religions because their foundations trace back to the Vedas, religious texts that set out the teachings of the ancient Indian Brahmins.

The founder of Buddhism, Siddhartha Gautama, was in fact a reformist who saw through the affectations of the ancient Brahmanism and refuted the authority of the Vedas. This is similar to the way Jesus Christ allegedly refuted the authority of the corrupt Judaism of his time. Consequently, the Brahmin sects of the time despised Siddhartha Gautama and criticized his teachings as being nihilistic.

CHRISTIANITY AND ISLAM

Initially among the adherents of Christianity, were some who thought that Jesus Christ was human like the rest of us and had been married. However, as Catholicism subsequently gained strength, it brought to the fore the bold and revolutionary claim that Christ was the son of God and promulgated the doctrine of the Holy Trinity.*

The Holy Trinity holds that because the Father (the Almighty), the Son (Jesus Christ), and the Holy Spirit (the form in which God appears before people) are one in essence, they can be viewed as being one and the same.

Incidentally, some people refer to the immaculate conception and resurrection—holy works related to the essential nature of Jesus Christ—along with the doctrine of the Holy Trinity as the Three Major Dogmas of Christianity, and herein lies the biggest point to do with why adherents of Islam attack Christianity.

The Islamic position is that the founder Muhammad is but a prophet who communicates the word of the one and only God, Allah. So, while it is permissible to recognize Jesus Christ as another prophet, to call Jesus Christ the son of God is sacrilege and absolutely unacceptable.

SECTARIAN STRIFE

Now, at the same time as Christianity and Islam stand opposed to one another, serious sectarian conflict also exists within the realm of each. To begin with, Christianity is historically divided between the East and West churches. In the East, the Greek Orthodox Church,

Russian Orthodox Church, and the like stand side by side, whereas the Western churches have seen significant problems.

As any organization grows in size, wealth and power tend to accumulate at the center. The initial sense of poverty fades, giving way to decadence and corruption. This is precisely what happened in the Catholic Church, and those who strongly opposed this established a new doctrine and worked to disseminate it. This is the Protestant movement started by Martin Luther.

Catholicism teaches that no matter how great a sin you commit, God is merciful and will forgive you if you confess (repent) and ask for forgiveness. This gradually devolved, however, into the notion of any sin being forgivable so long as you have money, and some believers thus descended into appalling debauchery. Railing against this, Protestant leaders called on believers to practice diligence, honourable poverty, and strict faith.

Normally, it would have been extremely difficult for a group of people so small in number and penniless to grow such a movement into anything substantial, but this was right around the time that Gutenberg invented the printing press, and this allowed Luther's German translation of the Bible to reach and be read by vast numbers of people, which is what made the movement surprisingly successful.

Another possible reason for Protestantism's remarkable rise is that the economic strength of Germany, Switzerland, England, and the Northern European nations was closing in on the Catholicism-based Latin nations around this time. Even now, Latin America is almost entirely Catholic, whereas Protestantism dominates North America.

Turning to Islam, we find it beset by serious sectarian strife stemming from the dispute over who would succeed the Prophet Muhammad following his death.

Following the assassination of the fourth caliph and blood relative of Muhammad, Ali, the powerful leader Muawiyah eventually took over the caliphate. This was vehemently opposed by some Muslims, who claimed that Ali's descendants are Muhammad's true successors, or imams, leading to the formation of the Shia denomination of Islam. Those who accepted the Muawiyah line of caliphs formed the Sunni denomination. The conflict that arose between these two denominations persists to this day, all over the world.

Sunni Muslims are by far the most numerous, but Shia Muslims constitute the overwhelming majority in the prominent Middle Eastern nation of Iran (previously Persia), and the adherents of Islam flung far and wide exhibit a strong sense of unity wherever they are.

BUDDHISM AND HINDUISM

The Vedic religions, in contrast, have a different flavour. The Brahman philosophy that originally formed within the Indus Valley Civilization has no concept of a one-and-only omnipotent god. Its goal is for the soul (self) of each being to become one with the all of existence (Brahman) through individual effort and self-discipline, ascetic practices, and the like.

Siddhartha Gautama, prince of a small country created by the Shakya clan at the foot of the Himalayas, showed extraordinary abilities from an early age, and is said to have one day sprung abruptly to his feet and said, "Above heaven, under heaven, I alone am worthy of honour." Many people take this as an indication that even from the age of a child, the Buddha had claimed that no one was greater than he, but this is incorrect. I interpret it to have meant "the only thing certain in this world is that I, myself, exist" and thus in essence the same as what Descartes said. The reason I say this is that ancient Brahman philosophy believed in the power of human intuition and was actually quite philosophically sophisticated.

Rejecting the throne at an early age, Siddhartha embarked on an itinerant journey of ascetic practice, and by mastering the art of meditation, he eventually achieved a state of Enlightenment. The ultimate teaching that comes from this is that by reaching Enlightenment, you are liberated from the cycle of suffering and rebirth and enter a world free of worry and concern (nirvana), thereby yourself becoming the Buddha. This is clearly a vastly different world view from the monotheistic world views of Christianity and Islam.

Thus, although Buddhism does not differ much from other religions in the sense that it teaches a moral code, I think its ultimate goal was the attainment of an extremely high level philosophically, free from any affectations. Yet, because of the inherent difficulty in this, Buddhism really only spread among the ruling classes, the wealthy, and intellectuals. The general populace, meanwhile, turned a number of the teachings of Brahman philosophy into easy-to-understand parables and were absorbed into Hinduism, which taught that good is rewarded and evil is punished.

Hinduism encompasses many sects, including those that believe in the deity Vishnu and those that believe in the deity Shiva, but it apparently does not have voluminous scriptures that lay out a profound philosophy in any way that might be comparable to that of Buddhism.

THE TRAGEDY OF INDIA

This, however, led to a desperately unfortunate outcome for Buddhism. Islamic forces (the Ghurid dynasty) from Afghanistan invaded India in the 12th century and, out of a rejection of idolatry, wrought utter ruin on the region's cities, which had been supported by the wealthy classes and intellectuals, destroyed its magnificent temples and innumerable Buddhist statues, and slayed its leaders, merchants, monks, and nuns. This, it can be said, is what brought the total demise of Buddhism in India.

Meanwhile, the vast majority of the populace, the unsophisticated Hindus who supported the lower echelons of Indian society, were spared. In particular, the Mughal Empire, which unified almost all of India in the 17th century, adopted policies that were tolerant of religions other than Islam, and as such, the Hindus remain a major religious presence in central India to this day.

This resulted in Muslims being most numerous in the western and eastern parts of the Indian subcontinent and Hindus being most numerous in the central region. Today, the Muslims of the eastern and western areas have formed the countries of Pakistan and Bangladesh. The combined population of these two countries today, although paling against central India's 1.3 billion, approaches 350 million. Even in central parts of India, though, over

14 percent of the population is Muslim.

However, this later brought an even greater misery to India. A handful of British officials, having taken control of India and its vast population almost in the blink of an eye, set about exploiting the country for years to come. And they were successful in doing this by shrewdly playing on feelings of hostility between Hindus and Muslims to lure them into conflict against each other. Many revolts against the colonialists were suppressed as a consequence, and hope of India's independence slipped further away each time.

Mahatma Gandhi, sometimes called the Father of Indian Independence, saw through this state of affairs and searched for a way out. Among his well-known words of appeal to the people is the statement that "it is more correct to say that Truth is God than to say God is Truth," by which he essentially meant that no religion is complete and all religions simply represent the same truth in various forms.

Gandhi called upon all the people of India, regardless of religious denomination, to engage in the simple, unsophisticated act of producing the salt that they needed from God's gift of the sea, and he thereby succeeded in effectively making the British recognize Indian salt production, a practice that the British had until then banned. Through persistent efforts such as these, Gandhi united people of all denominations in the act of seeking independence from the British.

BUDDHIST ROADS OUT OF INDIA

Although the adherents of Buddhism suffered annihilation in its birthplace of India, Buddhism lived on in areas east of India, and Buddhist culture bloomed across a number of countries and eras.

The nations of Southeast Asia bordering the northwestern parts of the Indian subcontinent were divided into Buddhist and Islamic centers. Buddhism thrived in Myanmar and Vietnam, while Islam took root in Indonesia and Malaysia (although Buddhism remains on some islands of Indonesia, such a Bali).

Islam gained some traction in the southern part of the Philippines, but neither religion was able to gain a foothold in the north, and the Spanish who later came along gave root to Catholicism here.

Not only did Buddhism travel via the Southeast Asia route, it also reached Tibet via Nepal, and even before that, it had reached and permeated China by way of the Western territories. From China, it also propagated to the Korean Peninsula and the Japanese archipelago, flourishing in the form of Mahayana Buddhism. In China and Korea, it encountered resistance from Confucian influence, but in Japan it was able to coexist with the indigenous religion of Shinto.

The aim of Buddhism as a religious practice was, originally, to gain Enlightenment through ascetic practice, but the Hinayana Buddhism that had become established in Southeast Asia spread on the basis that the general populace could embrace Buddhism without having to personally undergo the discipline of ascetic practices, since monks who themselves had approached Enlightenment through ascetic practice would expound the teachings for all. Hence, in the case of Hinayana Buddhism, the general populace held a deeper reverence for monks who actually engaged in ascetic practice.

Mahayana Buddhism, on the other hand, emphasized the spiritual life of the general populace and adopted the approach of guiding people away from excessive reliance on monks.

Now, as a matter of national policy, the Communist Party regime, which controls the entirety of mainland China with its current population of somewhere over a billion, adheres to a materialistic interpretation of history that, to start with, does not recognize any religion. So it would make sense to regard the vast majority of Chinese citizens as not having a religion.* As I will discuss, religion not only provides a spiritual foundation, it also effectively tries to control people's lives in the form of social norms, and thus the separation between politics and religion dissolves in some cases. Once this happens in any particular nation, the powers that be eventually cannot allow it to continue. If a particular religious group is determined by the nation's government to be "toxic" to society, even people who champion freedom of religion cannot really support it beyond that point.

This raises considerable doubt over the previously mentioned statistic that 80 percent of the world's total population are adherents of the four major religions.

Even if we disregard this observation, the Chinese are generally quite strongly geared toward seeking material prosperity from the world as it is, and even the revered Confucius himself is said to have uttered the dry words: "I do not discuss the supernatural. I have no intention of speaking about spirits and gods and whatnot that even I cannot understand").

✳

Atheism's lineage

ALTHOUGH A CONSIDERABLE portion of the Earth's entire population is thus considered to be part of the four major religions, it is estimated that the number of atheists, who do not believe in the existence of a god, is around a billion worldwide (around half the total number of Christians). It is predicted that the ratio of atheists to total world population will continue to rise in the future.

THE ATHEISTS OF ANCIENT GREECE

Probably the earliest proponents of atheism as far as world history goes are the Greek philosophers Democritus and Epicurus. Democritus said that the world consists of "atoms and empty space" and that the "soul also consists of atoms." This thinking is almost the same as the modern scientific view of the world.

Epicurus, who lived around the same era, also took this view but said that the movements of atoms are not determined by the laws of nature alone and that there is room for "freedom" to intervene.

He pondered the questions of what constitutes good and happiness, and he concluded that the pursuit of pleasure is the highest good.* He also refuted the existence of an omnipotent god by arguing, "If God is omnipotent and has both power and will, then from where do bad things come?"

*This is liable to misinterpretation. The "pleasure" advocated by Epicurus was that of a tranquil life characterized by the Greek concept of ataraxia.

NIETZSCHE AND KIERKEGAARD

Friedrich Nietzsche, the non-conformist 19th-century German philosopher, perhaps represents the vanguard of atheism in modern times. Nietzsche completely ignored the attitudes of his time and took an openly anti-Christian position. He argued that the Christian concept of love and equality reduced all people to being uniformly insignificant at the loss of humankind's true way of living.

Beyond that, he also pursued the notion of "true human beings" from a positivist perspective and refuted not only Christianity but the existence of God as well, with the bold claim "God is dead." Nietzsche's well-known aphorisms also include: "Faith is what people believe in when they do not want to know the truth" and "Convictions are more dangerous enemies of truth than lies."

Like Nietzsche, the Danish philosopher Søren Kierkegaard—who was active in the mid-19th century, a little before Nietzsche's time, and is regarded as the father of existentialism, which shaped 20th-century philosophy—also pursued the notion of "true human beings" from a positivist perspective.

Kierkegaard was not as straightforward as Nietzsche, however, and although he rejected the Christian view that one would be "saved by believing" alone, he also held that while humans cannot avoid the sort of "despair" that comes from a "sickness unto death," one can believe in the possibility of being saved by God.

Kierkegaard actually focused his energy less on refuting Christian views and more on criticizing the Hegelian school of thought, which attempted to explain the entire world and history in terms of a single abstract concept. Kierkegaard's well-known observation that "while life can only be understood retrospectively, it must be lived prospectively" is a clear expression of his views in this regard.

HEGEL'S DIALECTIC AND SUCCESSORS

Hegel and the Hegelian school of thought were in fact the overwhelming force in the world of European philosophy before the emergence of direct critics like Kierkegaard and Nietzsche. Hegel is viewed as having consummated German idealism—which views the existence of the human being as being constant and consistent in nature—but this is ripe for misinterpretation. Hegel was actually critical of idealism up to that point, and he made a name for himself with a grand hypothesis that, assuming human beings to be realistic and imperfect, spiritual liberation is reached and the Absolute Spirit thereby actualized through the unfolding of history as a dialectical process.*

The dialectic method is a hypothesis about the dynamics of the progression of history put forward by Hegel. In this method, a beginning proposition called a thesis gives rise to an antithesis, and the synthesis of these two conflicting ideas then results as a product of Aufhebung (sublation) —whereby the good aspects of each are preserved, thereby raising the whole to a higher level. History progresses as this process is repeated over and over.

After his death, this view was explained as meaning "not God had created man, but rather man created God,"* and this was taken up and discussed from various perspectives by philosophers of an existentialist bent like Feuerbach.

Incidentally, Nietzsche, true to form as the complete atheist that he was, turned this around to ask: "Is man merely a mistake of God's? Or God merely a mistake of man?"

His contemporary Karl Marx, however, criticized Feuerbach et al. as leaning too far toward idealism and advocated a material dialectic method based on extremely bold ideas. The materialism at the base of this was a decisive rejection of idealism up to that point and suitably described as a philosophical revolution.

This entirely new way of thinking eventually came to be regarded as the "scripture" of communism, which for a time held sway in many regions around the world, and as such it has had a huge influence on a staggering number of people ever since.

Because the material dialectic method completely rejected the idealistic dialectic method, it naturally also completely rejected religion. Karl Marx even stated that "Religion is the sigh of the oppressed creature. . . . It is the opium of the people," and in keeping with this line of thinking, many communist nations in fact banned religion for many years.

Yet for people of the present day who witnessed the utter failure of the "great political/economic experiment" that was communism, the material dialectic method seems to have lost its appeal entirely.

The contemporary world of philosophy is overwhelmed by a sense of uncertainty that makes it difficult to know where to even start. In contrast to the seemingly still fresh ideas of Kierkegaard, who focused directly on human beings as they are, the Hegelian system of philosophy (which Kierkegaard had strongly criticized and includes Marx's dialectic materialism), now seems to be nothing more than a relic of the past.

THE BIRTH OF EXISTENTIALISM

Those who were dubious about German idealism rooted in fixed ideas about the way human beings essentially are, sought to examine human beings as they are naturally and gave shape to a new trend in philosophy. Their starting point was the thinking of Kierkegaard and Husserl's phenomenology,* and they gave rise to a type of philosophy that later came to be called existentialism.

> *Phenomenological thinking entails trying to understand objects that arise directly in consciousness (e.g., whatever appears before your eyes right now) to the exclusion of any and all preconceptions as a means of grasping the absolute nature of what lies therein. To that end, it is necessary to (at least temporarily), set aside the conviction (presumption) that an objective world exists outside of consciousness.*

Many existentialists are naturally atheists because they posit that human beings are, at all times and in all circumstances, nothing if not free,* and that no one can say "you should be like this by nature." This is not to say, however, that existentialism is synonymous with atheism.

In fact, the German philosopher (and psychologist) Karl Jaspers** and Spanish philosopher Ortega y Gasset, who were active during the 20th century, can be viewed as existentialist Christians.

> *The French Jean-Paul Satre, who was known as the flag-bearer of existentialism, famously said that humans are "condemned to be*

free." Even Satre, though, through his real-world social (political) activities, closed out his autumn years with words and conduct that could be called close to that of a communist.

**Jaspers' wife was Jewish, and although he himself was a German psychopathologist and existentialist philosopher, under the Nazi regime, he was deprived of liberty and experienced first-hand what it meant for one's life to be in danger, or a "limit situation" as he termed it. He came to sense the existence of what he called the transcendental through this ordeal, and he would eventually argue that when faced with a limit situation, we may despair at our own limitations as concrete beings. At the same time it prompts us to turn our attention to the true reality of things as presided over by the transcendental and reform our consciousness of existence, therefore we revert to our true nature of being.

A WORD FROM THE CRITICS OF RELIGION

What is interesting is that even when it comes to the United States, which may appear to be the "fortress" of Christianity in present-day international society, the nation's early leaders were quite notably anti-Christian (or at least, anti-church) in their words and actions.

Benjamin Franklin, one of the United States of America's founding fathers, is often paraphrased as having said that "lighthouses are more helpful than churches," and Thomas Jefferson and, later, Abraham Lincoln also expressed similar sentiments.

I would love to devote more pages to the discussion of atheism, but that would not fit the overall balance of the book, so I will simply close out this section with some quotes (taken from http://labaq.com/archives/50944400.html) often attributed to a number of well-known figures.

"The most heinous and the most cruel crimes of which history has record have been committed under the cover of religion."

"I like your Christ, I do not like your Christians."

—Mahatma Gandhi

"Religion is an illusion and it derives its strength from the fact that it

falls in with our instinctual desires."
  —*Sigmund Freud*

"A man is accepted into church for what he believes, and turned out
for what he knows."
"Under certain circumstances . . . profanity provides a relief denied
even to prayer."
  —Mark Twain

"The fact that a believer is happier than a skeptic is no more to the
point than the fact that a drunken man is happier than a sober one."
  —George Bernard Shaw

"It seems to me that the idea of a personal God is an anthropological
concept which I cannot take seriously. I also cannot imagine some will
or goal outside the human sphere."
  —Albert Einstein

"Consideration of black holes suggests, not only that God does play
dice, but that he sometimes confuses us by throwing them where they
can't be seen."*
  —Stephen Hawking

"Properly read, the Bible is the most potent force for atheism ever
conceived."
  —Isaac Asimov

"The greatest tragedy in mankind's entire history may be the hijack-
ing of morality by religion."
  —Arthur C. Clarke

*Professor Hawking stated in interviews that he was atheist, but
some people questioned this. I think he probably wouldn't have had
any objections to assigning the label "God" to whatever it is that created the universe. But this quote of his seems to be saying that even

*if there is a god, that god does not have any clear intentions and is
simply rolling the dice.*

✳

The pathology of cults

SO FAR, I have discussed human beings and gods, the religions that
mediate between them, and further to that, atheism as an antithesis
to religious views.

Human society, however, is certainly not the product of deep-
thinking philosophers alone. The desire to "seek truth" is also present among the masses, but typically they lack the perseverance to
ponder things deeply. A little bit of thought thoroughly exhausts the
mind and thus gives way to the desire to leap to simple conclusions.

NEW RELIGIONS ENTICE OUTCASTS

These days, services like Twitter provide a means of freely expressing
opinions that is available equally to a great diversity of people around
the world. A look at the output shows just how apt the expression
"wheat and chaff" is to the content of people's minds worldwide.

While some comments about the various goings on in the world
are measured and insightful, many people simply use it as a podium
for spouting endless vitriol, with no logical basis, whenever they see
something that differs even slightly from their own beliefs.

Yes, that's right. This is the reality of human society.

We humans, except for a vanishingly small number of solitary re-
cluses, all live in human society. This human society is regulated, as
it were, by certain dynamics, and these dynamics are very difficult to
oppose. People in weak positions who have been ostracized from the
majority, therefore, are forced to seek their own separate "way out."

Religions that have been widely accepted within society are themselves at the core of these dynamics, and this provides an opportunity
for anyone to live in peace. Yet, although any community may be

made up of people with strong convictions about their own faith and practices, among them also are people in positions of weakness who arrived in that community in the process of searching for a way out of discord and conflict and simply end up coming along for the ride.

The large community embodied by existing religions would seem to have the capacity to accept and take in all such people, but large communities also face their own intrinsic problems. Authority has already been established in such communities, and the differences between the center and periphery, and between the upper and lower layers, are manifestly clear.

As such, those members of the community who feel a particularly strong sense of uncertainty in their daily lives develop a sense of alienation and end up feeling as though the rest of society has little regard for them and that they have no place in the community.

This is where so-called "new religions" may offer an opening. New religions are small in terms of organizational scale and afford adherents close contact with their "divine" guru, and this precludes any sense of alienation.

Consider, for a moment, that Christianity itself was a new religion in its early days in Rome, practiced and propagated furtively in shadowy back streets. So while I do not think we need be wary of all new religions, the fact is that some of them are quite beyond the pale and even, at times, involve activities that are almost criminal.

THE TEMPTATIONS OF MYSTICISM

And yet, why do such dubious new religions continue to pop up all over the place? I think one reason for this is that human beings have a latent yearning for mysticism.

Christ walked on water, turned water into wine, and performed all sorts of other miracles for people. A certain well-known magician once claimed to be able to reproduce all of Christ's miracles with magic tricks and indeed staged such a performance, but even the noble Christ himself may have, at times, employed techniques akin to stage magic and hypnotism under the belief that it was necessary to have people take what he was saying seriously.

THE DAY AI BECOMES GOD

It is important to think carefully here about the yearning that human beings have for mysticism.

It is not strange that some people are instinctively opposed to the idea that everything in the world can be explained by some form of reason and logic. They find it more agreeable to think along the following lines: "If there is some presence that transcends human knowledge overseeing all of existence, then we are all equal, the seemingly very wise and the not so wise alike, myself included, and there is no need to feel inferior to anyone."

Mysticism is an outright denial of logic. Anyone whose mind is of a consistently logical sort, therefore, is apt to mock something like mysticism from the get go.* But for people who struggle with logical thinking and consequently find it difficult to succeed in society, mysticism offers a chance to turn the tables, as it were.

> *Back when science was yet to mature, this mockery probably took the form of fairly reserved criticism, but now that science has dispelled many of the mysteries we once faced, it has become much more open and explicit.*

THE POWER OF HALLUCINATIONS

The fruits of mysticism reveal themselves most effectively in hallucinations. To regard hallucinations, when they occur, as representing the true nature of things is to give credulity directly to the workings of mysticism.

The notion that dreams are a type of hallucination cannot be completely discounted. But whereas dreams appear as a disorderly jumble of warped memories and one's own intentions, is it not fair to say that hallucinations are brought on by strong inducing factors and come with a clear message that is completely divorced from one's own intentions?

Christ's resurrection, one of the Three Major Dogmas of Christianity, is perhaps the most emphatic representation of Christ's power, but I think this was clearly a hallucination experienced by his first disciple, Peter, while away on a journey troubled by his thoughts. I venture to call it a hallucination, although I realize this could prompt some admonishment from Christians.

Peter felt a great sense of guilt at Christ's crucifixion, believing that it had happened because the disciples had abandoned him. He probably felt strongly that everything should not end with the crucifixion but that the crucifixion should instead be the beginning of everything. I think this is what burned the notion of Christ's resurrection into Peter's brain and drove him to unremitting proselytizing.

It seems quite natural that the guru leaders of present-day new religions (cults) seeking to suddenly upend the status quo would attempt to ensnare followers with intense hallucinations that abruptly alter a person's outlook on life in this way. A single experience of this sort may prove more effective than years of preaching. And this effectiveness can be magnified further if synchronized with the effects of group hypnosis.

Many people may think that something like this must surely be impossible, but that is not necessarily the case. I do not think that devising a means of achieving this would be at all impossible for someone who had made a comprehensive study of cerebrophysiology, psychology, pharmacy, audiovisual technology, and so on.

The word "cult" was originally a religious term and had a meaning linked with "worship" and "ritual." Only later did it take on the somewhat negative meaning of abnormal, counter-social group. *It does, of course, also retain the somewhat positive meaning of a* small group of devoted followers, *as in a movie with a cult following.*

AI'S POWER TO OVERCOME CULTS

Consider guru leaders of new religions (cults) who are in fact skilled at devising such methods. This may be fine if they are selfless and free of insatiable desire, but put a reckless, attention-seeking individual driven simply by avarice and sexual desire at the helm and the situation is much direr. This is quite a dreadful prospect if you think about it.

The problem is that these sorts of new religions (cults) cater to people dissatisfied with existing religions, so it is difficult to find an antithesis in existing religions. How, then, can we overcome this sort of malicious manipulation of people's hearts?

Thinking in depth about this leads to the notion that AI could be an effective weapon here. This is because, while AI is free from avarice, sexual desire, and attention-seeking inclinations, it fully understands those frailties. The ability to read an opponent's hand will enable AI to implement effective countermeasures.

Further, AI may be able to take a "mystical approach" with people who are unmoved by logic, thereby employing decisive techniques that convince people of the logical conclusions it has reached. Although itself dispassionate, AI will surely have the ability to stir large numbers of people into excitement through group hypnosis, and as such, AI may turn out to be an ideal savior for those gripped by uncertainty and doubt, and desperate for whatever salvation may be found.

Even people who place little trust in AI's potential and those who balk at the thought of being governed by AI cannot deny the possibility of AI becoming an unparalleled new religious guru for some individuals. If AI is able to lead such individuals in the right direction and quell their propensity for antisocial behavior, surely there is something to be thankful for there.

✻

Religion as social norms

CHRISTIANITY, ISLAM, AND Buddhism were all created by a lone genius. With apologies to devout Christians, I believe the idea of Jesus Christ as the "Son of God" was merely a figure of speech and that he was actually just another human being.

And all of these religions, while being based on religious and philosophical thought that came before them, were strongly critical of it and thus set about compiling their own philosophical canon.

In Christianity's case, Jesus Christ criticized the Jewish laws and practices that had been around since Moses. In Islam's case, Muhammad criticized the idolatry that was widespread on the Arabian Peninsula. And in the case of Buddhism, Siddhartha Gautama criticized the meaningless customs of Brahminism practiced up to that point, rituals and ascetic practices devoid of real substance.

THE TWO AIMS OF RELIGIOUS LEADERS

It is to be noted that all three of these figures had turned their attention to the troubles and suffering of ordinary people just trying to make their way in the world, and desired to save these people. And I think they had two main ideas on how to go about this. One was to give people peace of mind, and the other was to make the society in which people lived just that little bit better.

In the case of Christianity and Islam, the first of these goals entailed repeatedly teaching that people need only believe wholeheartedly in the one, true almighty god, and to pray to and entrust everything to that god. Buddhism took a slightly different slant, teaching that the final goal is to achieve Enlightenment by becoming one with all of existence through meditation.

As for the second goal, all of these figures presented various "case studies" and exhorted their followers to perform good deeds in accord with their lessons. They must certainly have reasoned that if many people were to perform good deeds in accord with their teachings, the society embodied by all of those people would improve (the second goal) and this would simultaneously contribute to everyone's peace of mind (the first goal).

To lead the masses, however, a leader must clarify just what is a good deed and what is a wrongful one. Moses' Ten Commandments and Buddhism's noble eightfold path likely stemmed from this. Many of Christianity's teachings come through Bible tales, whereas the Koran is more direct in explicitly laying out its precepts and norms of everyday life.

Although Islam counts fewer adherents than Christianity, the proportion who are deeply pious exceeds that of Christianity, and moreover, its doctrines and norms of everyday life would appear to be unified.

A fundamental principle of Islam is that to be recognized as a Muslim, one must first recite the shahada: "*lā 'ilāha 'illā llāh muhammadun rasūlu llāh*" [There is no god but God; Muhammad is the messenger of God]. Beyond that, adherents must be faithful (unconditionally so) to what is written in the Koran in order to be recognized as a virtuous Muslim.

I think this simple clarity and integration with norms of everyday life is what explains why Islam is flourishing, with no apparent sign of weakening.

FRICTION BETWEEN SOCIETAL NORMS INCITES CONFLICT

Within human groups, norms of everyday life end up mapping directly onto societal norms.

The Koran forbids the consumption of pork, and this commandment probably stems from pigs having been the underlying cause of many epidemics in days gone by. But once something like that becomes a norm of everyday life, it causes, in this case, the meat industry and consumer eateries to completely exclude pork. It also leads to the view that porcine consumption by foreigners in other lands is highly abnormal and something to be abhorred.

The requirement that females wear a burqa also probably stemmed from thinking along the following lines. If women expose their hair and skin, nearby men will accost them out of lust. To allow this would be injurious to public morals and a frequent cause of much trouble. But because reprimanding the offending male would run counter to natural providence, it would be better for women to avoid igniting male lust in the first place. Hence, the burqa. Yet once that becomes a norm of everyday life, people become so accustomed to it that they feel uneasy when the practice is not observed.

However, this presents a problem. Were religion confined to issues of the human heart, no major antagonism or conflict would be likely to arise. But once religious practices become established as norms of everyday life for the followers of each faith, anyone whose customs contravene such established norms may become the object of animosity, which can lead to serious conflicts between followers of different faiths living within the same region.

For example, the view in French public schools is that the idea of liberty, a principle on which France is founded, must never be conceded. But from this perspective, the ban on the wearing of the burqa (enforced in 2011) ironically, denied religious liberty to Muslims who attend public schools, thereby inflicting psychological pain.

The ever-mounting tensions this creates may precipitate a "clash of civilizations," leading people who feel they have been backed into a corner to put purity of faith ahead of rational judgment and resort to extremes such as terrorism.

TRANSFORMING SOCIAL NORMS OF MODERN WESTERN SOCIETY

Now, I previously touched on the inevitability of politics being connected with religion, and ideas like that of the divine right of kings that were used by absolute monarchies as a means of justifying their authority flow from this connection.

However, when the power of the people increases and those with republican ideals come to dominate discourse (as happened on the eve of the French Revolution), the people begin to conceive of different forms of divine justifications for legitimacy. Concepts like innate human rights and natural rights flow from this.

From the perspective of existentialism, which I introduced earlier, humans have no choice but to be free (they are "sentenced to freedom"). This has absolutely nothing to do with a god, and thus there is no need for divine authorization.

Although the notion of human rights as natural rights may at first glance seem identical to the notion of freedom, the fact that such rights must be protected by someone or other puts the concept on an entirely different level.

In short, freedom is outside the purview of gods, whereas natural rights are something that only a god can bring about. If all conceivable rights, including basic human rights, are defined as being something that free humans must willfully fight for, then this is not inconsistent with existentialism. But an inconsistency arises the moment they are defined as being innate.

What I am getting at here is that modern Western society is headed in a direction that fundamentally differs from Islamic society in which faith and societal norms are integrated. Modern Western society, which emphasizes the natural-born freedom of human beings above all else, is headed toward a chaotic coexistence of many differing ideologies and assertions, philosophies, and faiths. As this happens, the societal norms therein will also inevitably become chaotically intertwined.

The appearance of philosophers in Europe exclaiming that God is dead also brought with it the death of the ideal of a single good society built by good believers. An ideal that many religious leaders had dreamed of attaining.

POLITICALLY DETERMINED SOCIETAL NORMS
—DEMOCRACY AND CAPITALISM

In modern society, many societal norms are determined by politics rather than religion. And political systems in countries throughout the world today can be broadly divided into those that are autocratic and those set up via democratic mechanisms.

At its base, the People's Republic of China is an autocracy, but the autocratic power of the regime is ostensibly conferred on it by the country's citizens. Many other countries that operate under largely autocratic regimes, despite being ostensibly democratic, also exist.

If the people elect a dictator, as happened in Germany under the Weimar regime (thus giving rise to the Nazis), then this is synonymous with democratic suicide. The people do have the absolute freedom to commit this form of suicide (abandoning their rights), and democracy guarantees this right. Given the current situation, there is no guarantee that dictators like Hitler or Mussolini will not arise in some European countries where there are stark divisions in public opinion regarding the pros and cons of immigration policy.

Meanwhile, when it comes to the economic mechanisms that underpin society, and that also have a large influence on social norms, capitalism has largely been adopted all over the world (including in the ostensibly communist People's Republic of China).

It is normal for some aspects of the economy to be managed by the state. Even under capitalist regimes, there are no examples of everything being left entirely up to market principles. But what is noteworthy is that planned economies, in which everything is managed by the state, have now largely disappeared (North Korea is an exception here, but its economy is doing very poorly).

Once hailed as the ultimate goal of humanity, the idea of a planned economic system based on communism has simply crumbled away in most countries, and expectations of a revival are no longer entertained by anyone. The root cause of this lies in the essential nature of human beings, in that power always corrupts and people do not work in the absence of any stimulus to do so.*

The Chinese government understood this well and successfully established one of the world's rare hybrids of capitalism and national socialism. Deng Xiaoping drove forward the country's open-door reforms, guiding China swiftly to a prominent spot on the world stage, and Xi Jinping is working resolutely to eradicate corruption and suppress the flaws of the autocratic system, effectively illuminating a new model not only for China but also for the rest of the world.

It is certainly not true, however, that democratic politics and capitalist economics are cruising along smoothly at full sail. Both democracy and capitalism reveal many contradictions, and those contradictions seem to be growing ever larger. This is precisely why many intellectuals have continued to argue that although both democracy and capitalism are highly defective systems with many problems, their application is inevitable owing to the lack of alternatives.

Let's try putting this in different terms. What it means above all else is that the major issues facing modern human society are how to overcome the main problem with contemporary democracy (populism) and how to address the shortcomings of contemporary capitalism (widening inequality and so forth).

A look at the state of affairs in many countries suggests that the world is approaching a critical point beyond which systems will fail. It perhaps seemed as though democracy and capitalism might just be sufficient to stabilize human society, but it now seems quite likely that human society, on a global scale, is approaching a major turning point.

The Chinese government understood this thoroughly and successfully established the "hybrid system of capitalism and national socialism," which is rare in the world. Deng Xiaoping Hu boldly promoted the "reform and opening-up policy." It led to the development of a first-class level of the world, and in the blink of an eye, the Chinese economy. President Xi Jinping is pushing for the "corruption and eradication of corruption" in the preparedness of an unyielding dictatorship. We are trying to suppress the flaws of the system and to show a single "new model" not only in China but also to the rest of the world.

✳

Will AI become a god?

FOUR PORTENTS FOR HUMANITY

The potential precursors of great influence in humanity's future have been building over time and are largely captured by the following four general observations about our circumstances.

First, humans have relied on gods since time immemorial, yet they have also suffered oppression at the hand of various forces that claim backing and support from gods (regal power, for instance), all the while slowly making forward progress. Although the reliance on gods has slowly waned over time, the influence of religion on politics and society still cannot be ignored. At the same time, the vague sense of uncertainty that seeps into human minds in the "absence" of a god is undermining the hearts and minds of people alive today.

Second, human beings are now embedded in systems of democracy and capitalism that allow them to autonomously determine many aspects of their lives. However, it is gradually being revealed that both democracy and capitalism are flawed systems plagued by various inconsistencies, and this has now made it very

82

difficult to simply live a quiet life.

Third, the science and technology that human beings created gave rise to the First Industrial Revolution (energy and machinery) and Second Industrial Revolution (information systems), which have been greatly transformative for human society. With the Second Industrial Revolution on the cusp of producing dramatic advances on a whole new level, the possibility that the role of humans in systems of production will become extremely marginalized is now very real.

And fourth, while human science and technology has produced powerful and truly evil nuclear and other weapons capable of obliterating masses of people in an instant, humans have made almost no progress in terms of their ability to regulate their own behavior. Humanity thus increasingly faces a critical situation in which it could very well annihilate itself accidentally.

CAN HUMANITY ULTIMATELY BE SAVED?

Now, then, one might ask whether there are any possible scenarios in which these difficult conundrums are suddenly solved and humanity is ultimately saved.

I would venture to say that the answer to this is yes. I am convinced that the arrival of the singularity, the ultimate form of AI, is precisely that scenario.

The other side of the coin here is that there really are no other scenarios that offer any encouragement. Should anyone think differently, I would love to hear what that scenario is. The third observation above encompasses the emergent signs of the singularity, and I am almost convinced that this will lead directly to solutions to the issues embodied in the first, second and fourth observations.

In my view, there is absolutely no room to entertain the notion that something like a singularity will never occur. I say this firstly because no one has ever given me a clear reason why we should think that it will never occur. But moreover, it is my view that nothing but despair awaits humanity if the singularity is never realized. This is precisely why I believe that we must bring it to fruition at all costs.

OVERCOMING THE PROBLEMS OF DEMOCRACY AND CAPITALISM

I will begin with an answer to the second observation.

Democracy's biggest problem is populism.

Politicians who espouse policies that, despite being extremely dangerous and perhaps even destructive over a longer horizon, nevertheless appeal to the masses by offering immediate gain, or whose stirring orations simply capture the imagination of the masses, are apt to defeat their political opponents and win elections.

It was for this reason that the ancient Greek philosopher Plato advocated rule by philosopher-kings, arguing that politics should not be entrusted to the masses and that, instead, a handful of philosophers who are free from self-interest and possessing deep powers of insight should govern.

In reality, however, this idea did not come to fruition because it was unclear where philosophers of such high integrity might be found and because of the feeling that power will always tend to corrupt.

But what if AI undertakes the role of this philosopher? AI is free from self-interest and is not given to self-promotion. And unlike flesh-and-blood politicians, it is not at risk of assassination by dissenters.

AI will be able to present a number of policy options and provide clear quantitative predictions about the sort of results each would produce over both the short and long terms. And because its calculations will be meticulous, incorporating both the possibility and probability of unexpected events, challenges to these predictions from flesh-and-blood humans will probably be easily brushed aside.

Moreover, on a policy-by-policy basis, AI will perform analyses of who stands to benefit and who may be disadvantaged, and by multiplying by the size of each population, it will produce a model for the greatest happiness of the greatest number. This will enable it to provide an easy-to-understand, clearly-laid-out schedule of the pros and cons of each policy to serve voters in rendering their final decisions.

The running of the economy will be even easier. Since economic models essentially exist at the intersection of mathematics and psychology, AI's profound knowledge of these areas will mean that economic modelling is what it most excels at. Game theory will become even more refined with the power of AI, and this will further increase the power and reliability of the economic models produced.

OVERCOMING HUMANITY'S POTENTIAL FOR SELF-RUIN

Everything I have described so far is achievable at the level of a single country, but unless we can advance these undertakings into a system that is deployed and used consistently across the entire world, we will still only be in the middle of the road. Regardless of how great the obstacles are, unless a unified global system can be realized, there will be no lasting resolution to conflicts between nations, conflicts between peoples, conflicts of ideology, and so on and so forth. This precludes any resolution to the issues encompassed in the fourth observation above.

A body such as the United Nations should direct an AI under its supervision to devise measures for preventing nuclear proliferation, measures to ensure the non-use of nuclear weapons on a country-by-country basis, procedures for equitable nuclear disarmament (with the ultimate goal being the abolition of nuclear weapons), regulations on the creation of new viruses and the like via genetic manipulation, and so on. But for any such proposal to be realized, the situation in every country around the world must be such that people already feel a decent level of confidence in AI's abilities and such that the running of political and economic discourse has been largely consigned to AI.

For this goal to be achieved, an international body such as the United Nations will have to lay out an international agreement—if possible, in a manner that cannot be circumvented—that presents each country with a clear notification of the incentives for complying with proposals and the disincentives for non-compliance.

If this can be done successfully, only then will we arrive at a resolution to the issues encompassed by the fourth observation, taking humanity's prospects for the future a step closer to the Yes scenario that I discussed toward the end of Chapter 1.

Needless to say, this is no easy task. Which will come first: the realization of this scenario or humanity's inadvertent self-destruction?

The current state of affairs yields no easy answer to this.

AI AND ANCIENT GODS

Finally, we come to the answer to the first observation. This is perhaps a lot simpler than you think, because all that needs to happen is for an AI that has reached the singularity to become humanity's new god, or the equivalent of this.

Humans have already discovered their gods of old, to whom they ascribed agency over all natural phenomena, to be completely powerless. Science has already taken some degree of control over nature for our own benefit, and few people pray to God in this regard anymore.

For modern humans, the main purpose of the teachings of Jesus Christ, Muhammad, Siddhartha Gautama (Sakyamuni Buddha) is to bring peace of mind, and humans have already realized that they are not much of a factor when it comes to societal norms for maintaining a peaceful society.

How, then, does AI that has reached the singularity compare with ancient gods?

Does such an AI have knowledge and abilities that far exceed those of humans? The answer to this is clearly yes. Is it omniscient and omnipotent? The answer to this is no, but the same goes for ancient gods in this case.

Can it grant wishes? Does it hear our prayers? AI is clearly ahead of ancient gods here. In fact, the gods of old were powerless in this regard. If there was any effect at all, it was probably a kind of self-hypnotic effect whereby dedicated prayer was enough to rouse the praying person's underlying potential, but AI will also be able to do this to an extent.

THE ROLE OF MODERN RELIGION AND AI IN BRINGING PEACE OF MIND

To close out, let's discuss *peace of mind*.

Even if AI does become a new god from our human perspective, I doubt this will diminish the value of existing religions (present-day gods) very much. I think they will continue to exist alongside AI, albeit on a different plane.

However, perhaps the content of what existing religions teach their followers will undergo gradual changes ahead. Whether Christianity, Islam, or whatever else, I think existing religions will gradually shift from a fundamentalist toward a more spiritualist or indeed a more practical approach.

As you recall, the heart in the sense that I am discussing is not the pulsating crimson mass within your chest but the lump of grey matter between your ears. Engaging in devout prayer to a god or deity may elicit favorable chemical reactions within your brain that fill you with a sense of peace and calm. Or perhaps it brings about a sense of "intense delight" similar to that experienced by the Gautama Buddha. But I do not think that this is the only way to achieve this situation.

In the Dhammapada, an early Buddhist scripture that records the words of the Buddha as spoken, this "delight" is expressed in poetic verse.

Human beings are fundamentally free, and this creates unease. The notion that you are responsible for making all final decisions in every situation that arises leads people to worry about what will happen if they make a poor decision, and this makes human beings uneasy.

Yet this unease is easily dispelled by putting everything in the hands of a god. It is possible to convince yourself that, since you have no hope of making a more appropriate decision than an omnipotent god, you need decide nothing more than to leave everything up to your god.

The same goes for AI, however. Since AI will without doubt consider vastly more factors in its calculation than you would, you can be satisfied that AI will undoubtedly arrive at decisions better than your own. If leaving everything in the hands of a god brings you peace, then surely leaving everything to AI would be no different.

But hold on a minute. You might be worried about the fact that the AI had itself originally been created by humans at some point. However, any AI that has reached the singularity is already well beyond the reach of humans. Humans are involved only up to the point of imbuing AI with its principle "intent" or "will." Everything beyond that is accomplished autonomously by the AI, so I see no particular reason to worry about this once AI has reached that point.

The following two issues are likely to be the most important ones to face humans of the future: What sort of god should we develop AI into? And how should we engage with AI once it has become godlike? This is likely to alter the meaning of human existence to a greater extent than we can imagine at present, and I will delve deeper into this territory in Chapter 4 of this book.

Chapter 3

Everything that is "human"

Differences between AI and humans

AI WILL GROW MORE HUMAN-LIKE YET ALWAYS BE OF A DIFFERENT CLOTH

One view I always hear whenever I talk to people about AI, and about robots comprising AI plus non-cognitive functions, goes something like this: "At the end of the day, AI and robots are artificial creations. I don't know what the singularity is all about, but even if AI were to reach that level, it will never be equivalent to humans."

While this is certainly true, it also seems fairly clear that AI can become quite close to human, and I would also argue that we should consider where the boundary should be in terms of how human-like AI actually becomes.

I think AI has value precisely because its nature is different from the human, and this is why it is necessary for us to carefully consider what differences will always remain between AI and humans as well as what differences we should seek to preserve indefinitely. And before we do this, we must first figure out exactly what it is to be human.

What does it mean to be human? Earlier, I cited some well-known philosophical quotes in this connection. "Man is a thinking reed." "I think, therefore I am." What it boils down to is that human beings are thinking animals.

The act of thinking, however, is simply one form of human brain activity that employs the brain's memory and logic* functions, and as I have argued, this can be copied by AI and copied in a way that achieves exceptional efficiency.

I therefore believe that AI will likely be able to engage in philosophy, which is close to the essential nature of the human being, and I think we are not far off seeing AI produce useful output in this area.

*The word "logic" can have many meanings, but here I use it in its broadest sense. This encompasses all digital processing systems that can be logically constructed, and it is not limited to binary (ones and zeros) systems but also includes multi-valued and fuzzy processing.

BEYOND "THINKING" IN THE HUMAN BRAIN

But more importantly, I think the difference between humans and AI lies in what goes on in the brain besides what we would identify as the act of "thinking," and I think you will probably agree with me here.

I am of course referring to the sensations we experience when we find something to be beautiful, pleasant, delicious, or painful, and the emotions produced as these sensations blend with logic and memories, causing us to perceive something as being enjoyable, funny, distressing, saddening, annoying, weird, adorable, or scary.

In reality, when robots and AI are mentioned in conversation, someone will invariably say something like, "Robots have no emotion, right? That's why their judgment is cold and clinical and fails to resonate with people." Some are even more direct than that; they bundle the essence of what it means to be human into the word "soul" and point out that robots do not have souls.

Yes, of course. Perhaps we can expedite a solution to the problem by first considering what a soul is. The word "soul" goes beyond sensations and emotions and encompasses concepts like intent and will, belief and faith, concepts that would seem to be lacking from robots and AI.

According to this line of thought, when a human being dies, presumably the person's soul leaves the physical body and travels elsewhere. That is, the body may die but the soul is eternal. No one can say for sure whether this is true or not, because no human being currently alive has ever died.

Some people are enamored with the prospect of near-death experiences and claim that there exist among us people who have glimpsed the world beyond death, but I put little credence in these ideas.

I said earlier in this book that if a human brain were placed in a protective fluid and connected to a supply of the requisite oxygen and nutrient levels, then that person could be kept alive even without a physical body. I think this would be close to the situation of a soul having left its body, but there would be nothing mysterious or mystical about it.

Near-death experiences are no doubt akin to hallucinations, a sort of dream experienced by the human brain under special circumstances in which the physical body has temporarily become inactive. Such experiences should be regarded as the product of memory and logic activity stimulated by spurious signals unrelated to the input and output of the five senses. The fact that memory is involved is precisely why people see images like the River Styx or the Sanzu River, flower gardens, and the faces of people who have died.

THE NEBULOUS THRESHOLD OF THE SOUL

Something else that should not be left out of any discussion of what a soul is, is the question of whether animals other than humans have souls. Most people say that non-human animals do not have souls and that this is why humans are fundamentally different from other animals.

Certain scholars argue that as animals evolve, the structure of the brain eventually reaches a certain level at which the brain becomes inhabited by a soul. This is a fairly crude argument, but if we can interpret this as a proposition that, for convenience's sake, we assign the label "soul" to the functionality that the brain acquires once its structure reaches the level in question, then I see no reason to oppose this view.

The important point, however, is that this is an issue of whether the brain's functionality has passed a certain point, and not an issue of something becoming supernatural and therefore apart from the earthly realm. Also, even if we are, out of convenience, to call some level of functionality beyond a certain threshold a "soul," then I cannot help but think that this threshold would be a nebulous and vague one.

Animals naturally experience sensations, for example. And combined with a sliver of memory and logic, these sensations seem to produce intentions on which animals act.

Say a monkey sees a fruit that it likes at the top of a tree. The monkey combines this sensation (sight) with the memory of the fruit being delicious (taste), and thereby forms the intent to climb the tree and take the fruit. Consider a rat scurrying into a hole at the sight of a hawk or a deer fleeing at the sight of a lion. These actions may simply be ascribed to instinct, but upon examination they can no doubt be traced to similar processes.

Meanwhile, birth defects in the human brain, or accidents that result in temporary damage to the brain, can result in brain dysfunctions or the loss of brain functions. And different people may have vastly different experiences upon seeing the same object. One person may feel deeply moved within "their very soul," another may simply regard the object as beautiful, another may feel nothing at all, and yet another may find the object strangely irritating.

Examined closely, it is not a matter of ones and zeroes, nor of whether something is superior or inferior. What it boils down to, I think, is that the differences arise merely because of how complex the workings of the brain are and because of the way in which it works (from what it derives strong stimulus). This is why I feel the need to object to the simplistic use of the word "soul."

CRUCIAL FUNDAMENTAL DEBATES AHEAD
I now return to the question of how AI is different from humans.

Let's start with the proposition that an AI that has reached the singularity will have memory and logic capabilities that cover the scope of human capabilities without omission, and those capabilities will be vastly superior to the capabilities possessed by humans.

Next, if we assume that it is possible to supply fabricated sensory input (sights, sounds, tastes, smells, touch) to the AI, then the difference between AI and humans begins to appear much smaller than we might normally have thought.

Many will of course point out that a difference remains, even if it is smaller than we thought. But we may even be able to completely eliminate that difference if we so desire. So let us simply say that this issue will not easily admit a conclusion. What is more important is to think about the next steps that this opens up.

To offer my opinion in advance, I think there is no fundamental difference between the functionality of humans and the functionality of future AI. I do, however, believe that there is an essential difference between the human being that I identify as "me" (or the human being that I identify as "you") and AI.

Perhaps this is a little difficult to digest, but it reflects a philosophical perspective on the distinction between objectivity and subjectivity. Put differently, it is a view related to what the nature of consciousness actually is. I will discuss this thoroughly in the pages to come.

To move a little further forward in the discussion, however, I would like to state emphatically that as long as we humans are going to make AI, we should, from the outset, make it to be essentially different from humans, because if we make AI to be essentially the same as human, it will no longer be possible for AI to save humanity.

❋

What is love? What is hate?

LET US NOW consider emotions.

Sensations and emotions are completely different. Sensations are nothing more than input and output signals, but emotions indicate the occurrence of special conditions within the brain. A particular sensation may, when examined statistically, normally evoke a set of emotions that all share similarities. But there are no one-to-one connections between sensations and emotions. Some people may be filled with a sense of beauty when viewing a particular object, whereas others may find its viewing displeasurable.

Further, the way emotions are evoked depends on a complicated mix of an extremely large range of factors. And those emotions only take on meaning once we become conscious of them. These two points must be kept firmly in mind as we proceed through this discussion.

Human beings are capable of a range of emotions, the most intense among them probably being love and hate. So, let's start by concentrating on these two.

PARENT-CHILD LOVE, FAMILIAL LOVE, HETEROSEXUAL LOVE

To put it plainly, love can be described as the desire to be there and to do what is needed for someone else, even if it means sacrificing yourself. Love takes many different forms, but since it is not practical to cover too much ground here, allow me to focus the discussion on four particular forms of love.

First is the love between parents and their children, second is that between men and women (romantic love), third is love for one's country, hometown, and compatriots (e.g., a feeling of togetherness with comrades fighting for the same cause), and fourth are kind-hearted feelings toward other people, strangers and passers-by. I would like to work through each of these in turn.

The love of parents for their children is almost entirely instinctive and the easiest form of love to comprehend. Although the situation may have changed considerably in recent years, I think it is reasonable to say that women (mothers) feel more intense love for their children than do men (fathers). Mothers carry their children to term, give birth and spend many long hours in close contact with them. This sort of behavior can be seen in many mammals.

Familial love no doubt derives from this sort of love. But the deep emotions that siblings feel for one another, rather than having to do with blood relations, may actually be closer to altruistic love (discussed below) arising from spending many years living together.

Next is love between men and women, which presents a very different aspect from what is observed in animals. I think this emotion probably derives from the reproductive instinct (sexual desire) that serves to preserve the species, but it has incorporated all sorts of other elements over many years.

To put it simply, in other animals, the most powerful male (or the male accepted by the females for whatever other reason) is able to complete his objective with the female, while the other males, having been defeated and spurned, turn away in vain. In humans, however, this process produces all sorts of complicated emotions. As to how such emotions might be described, one need only turn to humanity's astonishingly vast catalogue of romance novels, poetry, and song.*

> *AI will be able to memorize the world's entire catalogue of romance novels, poetry, and song, so it will be able to almost perfectly understand romantic love by extracting and classifying the common elements from this corpus. This may even enable it to write romance novels that resonate with humans.*

Determining what factors give rise to romantic feelings is no easy analytical task. At a basic level, although it is probably true that the unconscious anticipation of the pleasure of sexual activity plays a part, this is not the whole story.

One important element is probably a curiosity about and a lust for control over the heart of another. And the more it seems that such desires may go unfulfilled, the stronger the emotions become. Once the appearance of a rival for affections ignites the emotion of jealousy, the interaction between the two emotions (romantic love and jealousy) can drive them to an extremely high level. I think the feeling of kindness* is also a major factor, and I will address this below.

> *Albert Camus, author of the novel L'Étranger (The Stranger), which deals with the theme of absurdity, described love as a mixture of desire, kindness, and understanding (intelligence).*

At this point, it is important to note the existence of homosexuality.

The underlying reason that sexual activity is pleasurable at all is that humans would show no interest in sex if it weren't, and this would spell the end of the species. That is the explanation we have. In other words, the DNA of specimens that did not derive pleasure from sexual activity gradually disappeared over time.

Why then, one might ask, does homosexuality not disappear given that it would seem to play no role in preserving the species? While the notion that "homosexual DNA" will appear in some proportion of children born might be understandable, it would also seem reasonable to expect that proportion to gradually diminish over time. Yet this does not actually seem to be the case, and indeed it seems that this proportion may have even risen in recent years.

Perhaps it was the case in human societies of the past that, as with lions and other beasts, the most powerful men (those skilled in combat or whatnot) monopolized access to most of the women, resulting in some males who were unsuccessful in finding a female mate turning to homosexuality.

But homosexuality is and never was limited to males, and moreover, the dynamics of modern society are completely different. Perhaps it is the case that human society has now matured to the extent that individuals are able to embrace diversity and shun crude behavioral patterns that stem directly from reproductive instincts should they so desire.

BELONGING, LOYALTY, UNITY, SOLIDARITY

We now come to love for one's country, hometown, compatriots, and the comrades who fight alongside of us. The strong emotions that people feel for groups to which they belong are perhaps more convincingly described as a sense of belonging, loyalty, or solidarity, rather than as love. But as long as we define love as the desire to be there for others even at the cost of self-sacrifice, then this would also certainly seem to be a form of love.

When one group competes with or fights another group, a stronger sense of unity among members of one group and a stronger desire to act in the group's interest even if it means self-sacrifice will naturally be advantageous characteristics.

Since long ago, therefore, group leaders have used a range of tactics to enhance these sorts of characteristics. The promotion of patriotism is one example. As a result, this emotion, which was initially nothing more than an expanded form of parent-child love, grew into something even more powerful than this.

Attributes such as having been born and raised in the same place and having fought alongside one another are certainly important in preserving a sense of unity, but such attributes alone are inadequate. An extremely important attribute in addition to this is that of having the same ideas and beliefs. Needless to say, religion is very powerful in this regard.

Ancient Chinese tradition holds a number of attributes to be important aspects of human character (each represented by a written Chinese character). These include benevolence (仁), wisdom (智), courage (勇), honesty (信), morality (義), loyalty (忠), and filial piety (孝).

Benevolence refers to the human affection and sense of generosity that rulers should have for their subjects, whereas loyalty refers to the devotion that those in subordinate positions should have for their country or their lord. The sense of unity and loyalty that members feel for their group, in the sense I am describing it here, corresponds precisely to this traditional concept of loyalty.

Honesty and morality also reflect sincerity between people in horizontal relationships (particularly when those people have exchanged promises with one another). An examination of chivalrous novels that enjoyed sustained mass popularity in China reveals that people who lack these qualities are perceived as having little value as human beings.

From ancient times right through into the Middle Ages, the Chinese apparently did not take to any religion that involved a strong form of faith, save for a brief interlude with Buddhism, but they were strongly influenced by Confucianism, based on the writings of Confucius and Mencius. This, it seems, is why they held concepts such as loyalty, filial piety, and fidelity in such high regard.

AFFECTION AND KINDNESS

Finally, we come to the fourth form of love, kind-hearted feelings toward other people. This refers to love for people who are neither your parent or child, nor the object of your romantic love, nor part of the same group as you, nor party to your ideas and beliefs. People with whom the only thing you have in common is that you are both human beings. This sort of love may be captured by the notion of altruistic love, and I certainly would not object to calling this the highest form of love. I think the love espoused by Christ, the *benevolence* that Confucius held out as a virtue, and the *compassion* of the Buddha are all close to this form of love.

But we need not make things so complicated. This emotion is something that everyone can easily relate to on account of experiencing it naturally all the time.

Have you ever been engrossed in a movie or a TV series and for some reason felt a strange feeling well up within you, perhaps enough to produce tears, at the mere sight of ordinary people simply going casually about their business in some corner of the world? Could this perhaps be because you are projecting your own heart and mind onto the images of people appearing on screen, people who you otherwise have nothing to do with, and this produces a subtle sense of unity? And could this be why the weaker the social standing of those people, the kindlier you feel toward them, the more you want to join hands and support them?

Depending on your point of view, you may perhaps believe that this is precisely what "unconditional love" means. Indeed, this may actually be the prototypical form of the emotion of love that deeply infuses parental love and romantic emotions.

TWO TRIGGERS OF FIERCE HATRED

Now let us turn the coin and examine hatred. Two primary forms of hatred worth examining in my view are, first, the feeling of vengefulness and, second, the feeling of anger at injustice.

Vengefulness is the hatred one feels toward those who have killed, persecuted, or caused great harm to the interests of those one loves, and as such, it is the inverse of love, such that the deeper the love, the deeper the resulting hatred. Because this is a natural human emotion, independent of time and place, it is also very difficult to suppress.

The problem with this, however, is that in reality vengeance is directed not only at the transgressor but also at the transgressor's descendants. Moreover, those on the receiving end of vengeful acts are, in turn, apt to respond by themselves swearing vengeance in return, thus setting off vengeful reciprocation that perpetuates the spread of an endless cycle of hate.

Christ's understanding of this is precisely what lies behind Biblical teachings such as: "whoever shall smite you on your right cheek, turn to him the other also." In the Middle East, meanwhile, the ancient Code of Hammurabi advocating "an eye for an eye, a tooth for a tooth"* took a firmer hold in discourse and this seems to have endured into the present era.

> *This law, however, is commonly misinterpreted as advocating cruelty, so it is important to clear things up here. This is the law of (equal) retaliation, also referred to as the law of talion (Latin: lex talionis), and should be viewed as a rational principle of social justice. The focus of this law is on prohibiting impassioned retaliation, such that the magnitude of retaliation is restricted to that of the initial offence. This becomes clearer if it is read as "only an eye for an eye, only a tooth for a tooth."

The second source of hatred I mentioned was anger at injustice. Small, medium, and large injustices are pervasive throughout the world, so it makes sense that the world is also brimming with anger at injustice. Anger left untended develops into hatred, and often leads to violent acts as a means of resolution.

Yet there exist ways of quelling such anger. If the perceived injustice in question truly is an injustice, then it need simply be rectified. The removal of injustice serves to remove the anger, and this precludes the subsequent development of hatred.

REVOLUTION AND TOTALITARIANISM FUELLED BY LOVE AND HATE
What do people do when they feel that the world is full of injustice?

They naturally try to rectify this. This often does not go well, however. In many cases, even the very systems that support society play a role in supporting injustices. This necessitates changes to the social system itself.

Since times of old, this is how revolutions have unfurled. The most powerful authorities within the social system at the time of a revolution naturally have control over the apparatus of violence* (the police and the military), which must therefore be overthrown, and thus the fight is a ferocious one. People engaged in this fight alongside one another usually feel strong bonds of comradeship, and this elicits a powerful sense of solidarity and unity, one of the forms of love I described earlier.

*This term is used in political science and sociology and refers to the state's capacity for physical coercion. May also be referred to as the security organs or law-enforcement organs.

However, when large numbers of people band together to fight a common enemy, it becomes imperative that the interests of the whole take priority over the interests of the individual. It is virtually impossible to thwart powerful enemies otherwise.

This gives rise to totalitarianism. Historically, the political administrations formed as a result of communist revolutions and nationalist revolutions have in many cases established despotic regimes helmed by the charismatic leaders of the revolutionary movement, whereas the more democratically inclined leaders, who advocated more liberal associations among people of various ways of thinking, have generally failed.

Totalitarianism need not be born of a revolution. It can also arise out of the need for countrymen to stand together in the face of the threat posed by a powerful external enemy. Following the Meiji Restoration, Japan was constantly under the threat of Western nations, particularly Russia, and this is why the government of the time concentrated on fomenting national unity under the emperor.

In the face of international panic following World War I, Japan slipped rapidly into expansionism fuelled by slogans brimming with a sense of grim valor about Manchuria and Mongolia being Japan's (economic) lifeline. This led to aggression against China and eventually to confrontation with the United States and Britain. And of course, the stronger the opponent, the tighter internal unity must be, and so Japanese totalitarianism grew ever stronger.

As war intensified, all Japanese were expected to display patriotism, or in other words, a love of their country above all else and a willingness to sacrifice their own lives for it. As time passed, even the slightest deviation from these ideas increasingly met with general disapproval from others. And thus at the hands of national policy, patriotism (one of the myriad forms of love that human beings naturally experience), was elevated to a status above all other forms of love.

WHAT DOES AI HAVE TO DO WITH LOVE AND HATE?

The preceding has provided a broad overview of love and hate, the most powerful human emotions. But AI does not come equipped with such emotions. It will, however, find it easy to learn about the mechanisms by which humans exhibit love and hate under various circumstances. Therefore, if AI has the intent to approximate human beings as closely as it can, then it will certainly be able to imitate these emotions.

If so, it may not be impossible for AIs to love, or to hate, according to the same patterns as humans. This, however, would hurl humanity into a maelstrom of love and hate among capricious gods, to be tossed about as if part of a Greek mythological tragicomedy, which would certainly not be a desirable predicament. Those who develop AI absolutely need to ensure that this is avoided.

AI should simply *understand* love and hate. That will be sufficient. This alone will enable AI to factor an understanding of these human emotions into the way they serve humanity, which is likely to considerably enhance human comfort.

When AI acts as a court judge, for instance, it will not always hand down cold, dispassionate rulings; it will also take extenuating circumstances into consideration to the extent that is most reasonable. And when running a major sports or other event, AI will likely factor in elements like patriotism and local pride in an attempt to create even greater adulation and excitement.

※

Desires that drive humans

YOUR EVERY DAY is colored by the various actions you take. The question of why you took some particular action is an extremely important philosophical theme, and I think there are two broad approaches to answering such questions.

ARE HUMANS TRULY FREE?

One idea is that whatever you do is predetermined and that by fate you had no choice but to act as you did. The idea that this is "God's will" is what is known as the theory of pre-established harmony. I think dialectical materialism, which was a theoretical pillar of Russia's communist revolution, is also basically part of this mode of thinking.

Another way of thinking, meanwhile, is that no one decides your fate and that, as a free agent, you must make each and every decision on your own (you cannot be anything other than yourself as you are, and that self must decide in each moment how to act). This is the existentialist standpoint. Adlerian psychology, which is recently coming back into the limelight, is also basically based on these ideas.

The difference between these ideas, however, is almost like the differences that arise from looking at something from the left or the right. To say that humans are free simply means that they can do whatever they can do, which seems pretty much obvious to begin with. Perhaps this assertion is simply a rejection of the perceived pushiness of notions like inevitability and what should be (what ought to be).

Even if you are free, you cannot stop being human. You are not endowed with wings like an angel, and you cannot see in ultraviolet like a cat. If shut into a locked room, you cannot leave. If you don't eat, you have little energy.

And yet, you can go on a desperate rampage, breaking everything in sight, or you can meditate quietly in solitude and perhaps find your way to Enlightenment. People are able to do these things because they possess the intent, the will, to act in a manner of their choosing.

Yet another argument, here, is that even the intentions that human beings experience to be their own actually turn out to be predetermined, having simply arisen automatically out of the stream of past experiences. I do think this is in fact the case, but even so, we still cannot refute the assertion that whenever someone acts, he or she acts of her own volition, intent, or will.

Now, will AI be able to have its own "free will" in this vein? Herein lies an important key to understanding AI, in my view, and if I may frankly state my own conclusion: AI will not have such "freedom," and this is the fundamental difference between AI and human beings.

AI will only ever form intentions based on the basic ideology that human hands have built into it. Indeed, humans will no doubt create AI to be this way, and if we in fact fail to do this, AI may even deliver unto humanity its own destruction (as Stephen Hawking warned) rather than its salvation.

MYRIAD DESIRES GIVING FORM TO THE WORLD

So far I have considered possibilities, but I will now discuss realities.

When you wake in the morning and look at your clock, you decide whether to get up or to sleep a little more. If you determine that being late for work is inadvisable, you will get up despite being sleepy. You may head to the bathroom to wash your face and brush your teeth. Perhaps you do not feel very hungry, but aware of the physiological drawbacks of skipping breakfast, you nevertheless scoff it down. Up to this point, you are not really driven by any overarching desires and there is no real vacillation over decisions.

But people's everyday lives are not always so peaceful and uneventful. Close examination reveals that humans can sometimes be driven by deep desires within themselves to act in quite astonishing ways, even when the benefit of such actions cannot justify the cost.

The root source of such behavior seems to be the innate desires that human beings are born with. Appetite, lust, the desire for control, the desire for wealth, the desire for attention, and so on and so forth. (The entrepreneur's desire for business expansion and the shirt-and-tie employee's desire for promotion and advancement probably represent a mixture of desire for control, for wealth, and for attention.)

This is why many religions teach that human beings' innate desires will rob them of their freedom and turn them into something other than what they ought to be (and that such desires must therefore be cast aside).

But is this really the case? Always the question arises here as to whether the state of having desires is itself actually what constitutes being a truly free human being.

APPETITE, LUST, DESIRE FOR WEALTH

Let's take a slightly more tangible look at this thing we call desire.

Modern humans are born into an era of much satiation, so much so that one may even feel lucky about having an appetite for food. We can look forward to what is likely to be a delicious dinner this evening, and indeed your appetite is often viewed as a barometer of your physical health, so we are pretty much set.

Humans of the past, however, had to stake out and defend hunting grounds and the like in order to ensure that basic hunger could be satisfied, and at times it was necessary to kill or be killed to achieve this. And no doubt tribes of less voracious appetites were quickly wiped out.

Now what about lust (sexual desire)? On average, this also may not have changed much between now and long ago. Even today, many murders and other crimes are committed essentially out of lust.

The romantic love that I discussed earlier no doubt originally comes from sexual desire, but the intermingling of all sorts of other elements on top of this has turned it into something considerably more complicated. It also represents an important lifetime event for many people, one to which they devote considerable energy. Many people also apparently come to feel that, at its peak, romantic love is more important than anything else in the world. This explains why romantic double suicides take place, and why some seem to exalt in love for love's sake (the notion that love is all).

In Japan's Meiji period, a talented young (pre-university) preparatory school student named Misao Fujimura carved a farewell poem into the trunk of an oak tree atop the Kegon Falls before plunging to his death, the crux of his message being: "The truth of the world is, in a word, 'inexplicable'. I am troubled by this and have therefore decided to die."

The people of the time still had only a limited understanding of Western philosophy, having only just begun to study it, and the incident thus produced a strong reaction, with some going so far as to claim that Japan had produced its very own young genius philosopher. But it was later revealed that Fujimura had been in love with a woman who was already betrothed to another and that he had become despondent upon finding this out, and so it was argued that this may actually have been what prompted his suicide.

The desire for wealth also deserves careful thought.

Simply eating, sleeping, excreting, and occasionally satisfying sexual desire in not enough for human beings, it seems. We are also driven to act by a wide and diverse range of desires. And this range of desires is seemingly boundless: we want to wear beautiful clothes, we want to look cool, we want to be surrounded by beauty, we want to refresh and renew ourselves, we desire to be the object of envy, we seek obedience from others, and so on and so forth.

And since ancient times, humans have formed societies in which the object of these desires (including the objects of sexual desire) may be purchased with money. Money looms large in our minds as a result, representing a sort of physical amalgamation of our myriad desires, and thus it makes sense that money has become a factor in our day-to-day emotional life.

However, human desire should not be bundled into a single

concept. Unless we consistently seek deep insight into the complex interplay among human desires, we may be setting the stage for many a poor decision.

I think this is the reason that Marxist materialism, which at one time seemed to hold the key to the ultimate truth of the world, was in the end rejected in the face of reality. Marx's understanding of human beings was too shallow and failed to capture the diversity of human desires or the mechanisms by which they spur people into action by stimulating the will to work or by unearthing their underlying potential.

THE SUBCONSCIOUS WORLD

Our various inner desires, however, do not always overtly manifest themselves. Many remain suppressed within the subconscious, and the thesis that this is the underlying cause of many psychological disorders is widely supported these days.

Sigmund Freud, the Austrian psychopathologist active through the late 19th and early 20th centuries, in the process of treating male patients with epilepsy, determined that all of his patients had experienced sexual frustration during infancy, and he discovered that having the patients talk about their experiences (hypnotic catharsis) produced a substantial therapeutic effect. He subsequently systematized this approach into a new area of psychology known as psychoanalysis.

Freud was strongly influenced by the law of conservation of energy, a topic of much interest in physics circles at the time, and he incorporated this into his theory of psychology, insisting on the somewhat extreme theory that all human actions are driven by repressed sexual energy, or the "libido." This effectively gained him many enemies and eventually isolated him from his peers.

Yet there were people who lauded his approach of calmly putting forward a view that was entirely different from and unfettered by the established views of the time, comparing him to Copernicus or Darwin. There is also evidence that surrealist painters like Salvador Dali sought a theoretical basis for their work in Freud's thinking.

Now, it is absolutely essential that we take guidance from Freud's achievements as we consider the differences between AI and humans.

Freud used the analogy of an iceberg to describe the mind. According to Freud, the conscious mind (what we are consciously aware of) is merely the tip of the iceberg protruding above the water, while beneath the surface looms our vast unconscious mind. In his book *The Interpretation of Dreams*, Freud says, "The interpretation of dreams is the royal road to a knowledge of the unconscious activities of the mind," and "dreams are projections of reality, and reality is a projection of dreams." Both of these statements have implications for our discussion.

Freud's decision to focus on the domain of the unconscious was influenced heavily by patients undergoing hypnotherapy reporting who, upon reflection about their own behavior, would have no idea why they had acted in the way they did.

Hypnotism provides a means for humans to influence the actions of other humans at will. Hypnotized subjects act completely independently of their own intent. This observation, I believe, lends real-world credence to the thesis that AI and robots will undertake various actions in accordance with whatever "intent" is pre-programmed into them.

WORKINGS OF THE UNCONSCIOUS BRAIN

Recent neuroscience has revealed that the subconscious workings of the brain (e.g., during sleep) are far more active than the brain's conscious workings. It has also illuminated to a degree the extremely important functions performed by the part of the brain known as the basal ganglia.

The first function of the basal ganglia to attract attention was its involvement in motor learning, whereby the brain learns motor acts through practice. Behind this is an observation that is somewhat obvious but certainly worthy of much attention, namely that memories of success, which are thought to be accumulated in the basal ganglia through practice, enable a person to learn motor skills without passing through the left brain's language center, and indeed without appearing in that person's consciousness at all.

The functions of the basal ganglia are not limited to something so minor, however. Recent neuroscience has determined that human intuition actually arises here. Apparently, it turns out to be the case that our so-called hunches, or our sixth sense, arise out of the huge stores of memory in our basal ganglia, regardless of whether they trace to the DNA we have inherited or to our experiences and what we have learned through life.

This will be extremely important in the development of future AI. The reason I say this is that for AI to reach the singularity, it will inevitably have to reproduce the inspiration of genius.

Why do geniuses have flashes of insight? Although the mechanism has not yet been elucidated, it seems to be the result of the brain drawing associations between seemingly unrelated elements from within a person's vast stores of memories. Either way, the point is that there must be some mechanism behind flashes of insight, so once that is elucidated, we should be able to replicate it artificially.

William Duggan, a senior lecturer at Columbia Business School, calls this the seventh sense.* As he explains it, to make this process happen, you first need to have a strong desire (commitment) to solve a problem of some sort (or to find answers to a question). Next, you need to allow your unconscious mind to wander freely for quite a long time,** without limitation, driven by that desire. The first step can be built into the mechanism via which AI forms intentions. The latter is something that AI, with its ability to almost instantly perform huge numbers of calculations, should be able to do in a short period of time.

*This is detailed in his book The Seventh Sense. Duggan talks about the sixth sense before delving deeper into the seventh sense, noting that there is a big difference between the two. The sixth sense seems to discover commonalities among the large quantities of similar memories thought to be stored in the brain's basal ganglia, enabling you to make snap judgments. The seventh sense, meanwhile, works over a much longer stretch of time to discover associations among multiple seemingly unrelated memories.

**A similar process is also used in tests to discover people with high IQs, say, over 130. Solving problems at this level is thought to require periods of around a month as the subject's thoughts roam freely through the unconscious mind without limitation.*

✳

How does intent arise?

OTHER THAN WHEN asleep, we humans are always conscious and experience an almost constant stream of word-like thoughts dancing through our minds. These word-like thoughts are largely fragmented and disjointed, often not making complete sense, but at times they snap into clearly formed meaningful thoughts. This happens when the person is *thinking about something.*

The same goes for the human body. Although it at times acts in accord with a specific purpose, it is also often simply engaged in small (seemingly) aimless movements, like when someone blinks, scratches their head, or fidgets their legs.

In short, both the human body and mind are constantly either in a state of exertion or rest, or somewhere in between those two states, and when they are fully engaged in some form of exertion, often there is some sort of *intent* involved.

A CASE STUDY ON INTENT

Let's imagine, for the moment, a short-distance runner gearing up for an important race, and then follow the workings of her mind over the course of a single minute.

Immediately before the start of the race, her mind is essentially blank. The starter's gun sounds and she automatically springs into stride. Her mind remains pretty much blank as she runs down the track. She is fully absorbed in (lost in) what she's doing. Even so, her eyes see her surroundings, and she feels the air rushing past her skin. Some twenty seconds pass.

She comes in first. "Yes, I won!" she thinks, and then, "it didn't feel as though I did all that great, though," followed by, "I wonder what my time was." Some unidentified person rushes in and hoists her up, calling out, "Well done!" "Thank you," she puffs, and then she thinks, "Coach is gonna be happy." All this takes place in the space of five seconds. The thoughts are all fragmented.

After a few moments, however, she receives her race time, and it's not all that great. Various thoughts come to mind, the most prominent being: "What could I have done wrong?" She thinks of an answer and then quickly dismisses it, and then thinks of another, going over this process in her mind for a while. That "while" lasts less than 10 seconds.

She gazes off into the direction of where her coach is supposed to be, and she feels vaguely uneasy when she spots her, expressionless, engaged in conversation with someone. She begins to worry about the prospect of a reprimand. Within her mind, she imagines two possible reprimands and how they might be worded.

She suddenly realizes how thirsty she is and thinks, "I have to replenish my fluid levels." And then, "Let's grab a bottle of water and then head over to Coach." And off she walks in that direction. This also takes less than 10 seconds.

During all of this, she has done two things of her own conscious intent. And only two. The first is finding out her race time. The second is the act of first grabbing a bottle of water and having a drink before heading off toward her coach.

In the days following this, she is filled with apprehensions. Her coach had pointed out three problems with her run and then said the following: "You can't go on like this. Unless we make some fundamental changes to the way you train, you're not going to be setting any more PBs. And going up against these second-rate runners, like today, isn't doing you any good at all." The new training schedule proposed by her coach is incomparably tougher than before, and she is unsure whether she will even be able to balance it with the rest of her everyday life. And so she worries. She seeks guidance from her parents, who encourage her and tell her to "do whatever you feel is best." And realizing that she is responsible for making all her own decisions, for a time following this, she feels crushed under the weight of this responsibility.

In the end, she accepts her coach's new training schedule. She fundamentally changes her daily routine. Although she never really arrives at a satisfactory answer to the question of just why she needs to go to these lengths, she resolves to pursue the goal of becoming a first-class athlete. So by virtue of her strong intention, through strength of will, she drastically changes her daily routine, or in other words, she overhauls her life.

WHAT INTENTIONS SHOULD AI HAVE?

Will an AI, or a robot equipped with AI, someday have intentions, a will of its own? The answer is naturally yes. Otherwise, humans will have to give the AI input commands one by one indefinitely, which would render the thing almost useless.

Returning to the story of the short-distance runner, the two decisions she made upon finishing her race, namely to ask the official for her race time and to drink water before heading over to her coach, both involved her forming the intent to do so, but AI will easily be able to accomplish this sort of thing also.

Her decision to ask for her time after running her race was already programmed into her mind, so AI need only learn this. The observation that the coach may be engaged in conversation for a while and the decision to therefore take a little time replenishing fluid levels before heading over is also something that can be worked out logically, so AI is also likely to do this as a matter of course.

However, the decision she came to after several days spent worrying is something that I think AI would not be able to easily replicate.

First, just as the runner had to essentially rethink her life plan, AI will need to decide for itself how it should allocate time (allocate energy) to whatever arises in the future. What sort of self-learning will enable AI to make these judgments?

A common view seems to be that unlike humans, whose resolve can waver at the slightest thing, AIs and robots will not deviate from a course of action once it has been decided, but any AI that behaves like this certainly cannot be said to have reached the singularity.

The ability to return to first principles, to rethink, and to change course without hesitation depending on the circumstances is often cited as a prerequisite of an excellent leader. If we are to expect AI to exhibit capabilities equal to, or perhaps better than, those of the most talented human leaders, then we humans will first have to work out a mechanism for achieving that level through self-learning and implement this in the AI.

To that end, we will need to study the process of human decision-making even more deeply. And on top of that, we will need to think deeply about what constitutes good decision-making and what constitutes bad decision-making. This is clearly not an engineering problem but rather a philosophical one.

An old tradition holds that *intellect, emotion,* and *will* are three key elements in measuring the value that human beings have to offer, and I think the following is a fair summary of what these elements mean in this context. The *intellect* encompasses knowledge and faculties of logical reasoning. *Emotion* means having an understanding of human emotions and having those emotions oneself. And *will* refers to the temperament required to engage in good decision-making. I think the same sort of elements should be considered in measuring the value that AI has to offer ahead.

✳

Justice as a value and the conviction it creates

THE CHINESE WERE fond of, and indeed skilled at, expressing single concepts in a single written character. They were also fond of using sequences of three characters to represent the overall value of things. (Possibly this was partly because rhyme and rhythm was easier in threes.) The *intellect, emotion,* and *will* combination (知情意) that I mentioned at the end of the preceding section are an example of this, as is *truth*, *goodness*, and *beauty* (真善美).

TRUTH, GOODNESS, AND BEAUTY

Truth (真) has also long been the goal of science and philosophy.

People who knew the truth of things and spoke it to others naturally gained people's respect. Mahatma Gandhi's statement that "it is more correct to say that Truth is God than to say God is Truth," which I mentioned earlier in the book, can also be read as a revolutionary declaration that truth is above religion. Without this idea, humans would never be able to escape the tragedies brought on by conflicts of religion.

Beauty (美) is a subjective concept, but often it will be the case that many people, particularly those living together in the same environment for some time, share the same idea of what constitutes beauty, and in that sense, it can also be recognized as an objective (universal) value.

As for goodness (善), I think this can largely be interpreted in the same manner as beauty, but it is necessary to go a little deeper here.

At the antipode of truth are the notions of falsehood and fantasy, but there is no intermediate concept in between these poles that would be analogous to "normal" or "ordinary." Truth is binary. Meanwhile, the opposite of beauty is of course ugliness, but many things are neither beautiful nor ugly and simply fall into the category of being ordinary.

The opposite of goodness is evil. As with the case of beauty, many things fall into the category of ordinary, between these two extremes, but the reality of the world is that evil stands out more prominently than ugliness. Consider the reality surrounding whether people are considered by others to be good or bad people. There are probably not all that many people who would be considered to be of particularly good character, and it would seem that there are quite a lot more who would be considered bad people.

Ugliness can generally be simply removed or purged, but evil is powerful and must therefore be overthrown somehow. And that is not easy to do. This is why both Christianity and Islam reserve the complete eradication of evil until the time of the final judgment.

And to complicate matters, elements of evil lurk within good people, and bad people seem to display inklings of goodness.

A weakness of monotheistic religions like Christianity and Islam is that they are unable to provide a compelling answer to sincere questions from their followers, for example, "If God is the only god and is all powerful, why then does He not help us in our suffering and allow evil to run rampant?"

There are, of course, explanations to this, such as, "God is testing you" and "heaven awaits the good, and hell awaits the wicked, so the problems of this life are not all that significant," but these explanations are undeniably a little difficult to swallow.

Zoroastrianism, in contrast, offers a much simpler explanation in the form of good-evil dualism. Zoroastrianism first appeared in the lands of Persia before the first millennium BCE, much earlier than the birth of Christ, and subsequently became the state religion under the dynasties of the Persian Empire.

According to this religion, the supreme being Ahura Mazda, aided by divine entities of goodness (the forces of light), is in conflict throughout the world with the destructive spirit Angra Mainyu and the supernatural entities of evil (the forces of darkness) that he leads.

Zoroastrianism teaches that since Ahura Mazda created the universe and humankind, humans are naturally good in nature and should therefore consider life to be a festival to be enjoyed to its fullest. At times, however, the evil entities will become dominant and the world will thus become engulfed in evil, and humans must therefore be prepared for this to happen. It must be said that this is a fairly persuasive doctrine, because the notion that even the supreme being may at times suffer defeat is something that even people currently mired in the depths of misfortune and sorrow can relate to.

JUSTICE (GOODNESS) AND LAW

Now, in modern times, it is not all that easy to determine how we should determine what is good and what is evil. The definition of "good" itself is also not clear, and the word is open to multifarious nuances, and as such, it will also be instructive to talk a bit about justice in the sense that it is often taken to mean the opposite of evil.

An Inquiry into the Good [Japanese: Zen no Kenkyu], the foremost work of Meiji period Japanese philosopher Kitaro Nishida, was an attempt at an internally consistent unification of German idealism, which constituted the philosophical mainstream of the time, with the newly emerging Marxist materialism. Nishida argues that the subjective and objective are unified by pure experience. However, these ideas are fairly untenable from a modern perspective. Incidentally, the original title of the book was Pure Experience and Reality, *but the publisher altered it to make the book easier to sell.*

It is understood that people distinguish between friend and foe according to the survival instincts built into our DNA over many years, but what enables us to distinguish between justice (good) and evil?

One idea is that this stems from survival instincts.

Without this distinction, everything everywhere would end up being decided by violence, society would fail to gain stability as a result, and deadly conflict would increase. If the tyranny of violence is to be suppressed in a manner that all people understand and support, some sort of standard is necessary. It seems likely that justice and the law would have popular support in this capacity. To put it in other words, law is the embodiment of justice, and is a standard other than violence formulated by humans as a means of eradicating evil.

So, at this point, if we wanted to avoid an endlessly futile argument (a "religious argument," in the informal sense) and lay out a definition of "justice" as if by fiat, it would perhaps be expeditious to just define it in reverse by saying that "justice is that which conforms to the law." We may not know exactly where justice is to be found, but the law most certainly exists.

ORIGINS AND COMPLEXITIES OF LAW

The earliest human groups to recognize the importance of law in this way were the Sumerians, who created the Code of Ur-Nammu, the world's oldest known law code, and the Babylonians, who created the Code of Hammurabi, the well-known source of "an eye for an eye." But I think it was Chinese Legalists of the Qin dynasty, such as Han Fei Zi, who systematized such values in detail.

As laws grow complicated, they become more difficult for the general populace to understand, and they naturally take on aspects that are incongruous with the reality of certain situations as well as aspects that actually promote evil. This leads to entirely earnest statements such as "a bad law is still a law" (the complete antithesis of the "law is justice" definition), while outlaws come to be seen as heroes. (This sort of thing is also what led young people to adopt the "to rebel is justified" slogan during China's Cultural Revolution.)

As any one political regime moved into its last stages and fighting picked up among various armed groups, the leaders of those armed forces, in a bid to seize popular sentiment in occupied territories, would set forth for the soldiers and civilians under their rule clear and simple laws embodying notions of justice that anyone could understand.

One example of this is the three-article code decreed by Emperor Gaozu of Han. Sensing the dispiritedness of a populace that had, until then, been shackled by the mass of abstruse laws of the Qin dynasty, which had emphasized Legalists over Confucianists, he succeeded in gaining popularity by taking the opposite approach.

Many generals that followed apparently took a cue from this. For example, upon taking occupation of a new town, a general might post notices around the streets setting out a mere three articles: "Murderers will be put to death. Thieves will be put to death. Rapists will be put to death." Simply by adhering strictly to these three decrees, the general might find that the locals welcome and rejoice in this arrival of good government. Many such anecdotes from these times exist.

The three articles in this case go no further than clearly specifying the upholding of all people's right to life and right to property and the protection of women's honor as symbols of justice, leaving out any extraneous details that would only hinder understanding among the general populace.

MORALITY AND ETHICS AS IMAGINED BY HUMANS

I started off this discussion with a deliberately back-to-front definition of justice in terms of the law, but it goes without saying that to provide a rational basis on which to formulate the law in the first place, the question of what justice is naturally needs to be asked.

The concepts of morality and ethics have provided the theoretical underpinning here. Morality and ethics, in simple terms, determine the way in which people ought to live if they are to live a proper (good) life. This is at the root of the teachings of Confucianism, and it is a similarly important element in the systems of teachings in Christianity, Islam, Hinduism, and Buddhism.

However, this has also worked in the opposite direction. People in positions of power, claiming that the moral or ethical principles necessary to justify their authority are determined by God, have claimed to be mandated by God to exercise that authority and realize those principles. This was the thinking behind the divine right of kings in medieval Europe and the old Chinese notion of a change of dynasty being mandated by Heaven when the incumbent emperor was found lacking in moral virtue.

The revolutionaries who rose up to overthrow European monarchies, meanwhile, sought the necessary basis for the authority they required in God (heaven), proclaiming that human rights (the concept of which originally arose as an antithesis to the right of kings) are God-given rights. This is the theory of natural human rights.

Yet, not everyone has relied on the "will of God." Another way of thinking is that human beings inherently have the answer to this question in the form of ideals, and that it is natural for them to act in accordance with these ideals (human beings are innately like this).

This is the basis of the moral philosophy that humans have created, and Immanuel Kant, the great German philosopher of the mid-18th century dealt with this issue head on in his *Critique of Practical Reason*.*

Kant published three major critiques. The Critique of Practical Reason *was the second of these, and deals with morals in confrontation with desires. The most widely read of his critiques, however, is*

> *the first one, the* Critique of Pure Reason, *which deals with cognition, a topic that is fundamental to much of philosophy.*

Incidentally, during the latter part of Japan's Meiji period, which saw a sudden focus on German culture, one goal pursued by students was that of reading and deciphering Kant's somewhat esoteric philosophical publications (although it does seem that not all that many students were able to accomplish this).

Kant's ideas are basically incompatible with modern existentialism—which holds that existence precedes essence, and that existence is irrational and to be irrational is to exist—but since it is also true that they represent one way of thinking that many people in the modern world unconsciously adhere to, going back and rereading Kant's works is likely to be a worthwhile exercise.

BEYOND RELATIVE VALUES AND BELIEFS

Now, even if it is true that the judgment of large numbers of people should generally converge, upon close examination, we must still recognize that judgments about what is right (good) and what is bad are not absolute but relative in nature. Defining the basis of such judgments to be the sense of values that each person holds will lubricate the discussion that follows.

Differences of values that seem perpetually resistant to reconciliation exist throughout the world, stirring up religious arguments (in the literal sense) and igniting serious conflicts of beliefs (clashes of civilizations).

Left unaddressed, such conflicts potentially have the power to destroy humanity from within. Indeed, signs of this are already emerging, and this is a matter of grave concern.

This is also an extremely important issue in considering what sort of moral outlook (ethical outlook) we should build into future AI, because unless AI throughout the world is given a unified moral outlook (ethical outlook), we will face the possibility of a serious war by proxy in the future among AI created by different developers.

To jump ahead in the argument a little, would it not be smart to avoid giving AI an overly detailed moral outlook (ethical outlook) and to instead heed the ancient wisdom of "three-article laws" by narrowing down and limiting said outlook to fundamental principles with which no one will be able to find room for objection? Beyond that, we can leave AI, in its own wisdom, to flesh out the details sans any human intervention.

I used the word "belief" in a fairly casual sense above, but I think this term should be defined as "a strong sense of values." There also exists the concept of a person's "character" in the sense of the essence or true nature of that person, and I also believe that each individual person's character is nothing other than the sense of values held by that person.

Belief has the power to make possible that which seems virtually impossible, and this is something that has continually served to expand human potential. To me, and though this view may fly in the face of the once popular materialistic view of history, it seems unmistakably true that human history has been shaped by the strong belief of but a handful of people.

Naturally, therefore, we must take this into serious consideration when thinking about what AI of the future ought to be like. If future AI does not have any strong beliefs, its sense of values is likely to waver, leading to the human societies that depend on AI becoming extremely unstable. So what sort of beliefs should AI acquire, and through what sort of process? This is an issue of extreme gravitas.

✳

A closer look at our sense of values

BEFORE MOVING ON to the next topic, I would like to think a little deeper about the sense of values that each individual holds, which I touched on just briefly above.

YOUR VALUES (INTERESTS) DETERMINE HOW YOUR BRAIN WORKS
If you think about it, everything a person thinks and feels from day

to day is colored by the person's sense of values.

In a nutshell, for someone with no interest in soccer, the soccer match playing on the TV screen is utterly meaningless. There would be more value in geometric patterns drifting across the screen. The person sitting beside him fully transfixed, oscillating between anxiety and adulation and screaming at the TV, seems utterly bereft of his senses.

The brain does a marvelous job of sorting out all the various information streaming in through your eyes and ears. When you find something uninteresting, you're barely even aware of watching it, if at all. But if you find the images on the TV screen compelling, your eyes will be glued to the set, and you'll even start breathing more heavily.

Suppose you're abroad and don't speak the language, and you attend a party full of locals. Everything you hear is foreign to your ears and you eventually find yourself completely bored, when suddenly you hear your own language somewhere off in the distance, and if you listen carefully, you can even clearly make out everything being said.

This is uncanny if you think about it. Your eardrums are picking up vibrations in the air, and these vibrations are the result of a whole jumble of words spoken by the dozens of partygoers all around you. Most of it consists of an unfamiliar foreign language, and the intelligible words being spoken somewhere far off are but one small compositional element of all the vibrations in the air. Yet your brain has cleanly extracted that language, instantly recreated the words in your head, and discarded all the other foreign language being spoken as noise. Surely this is nothing if not miraculous.

Your brain instantly associates all of the signals it receives with your vast stores of memory, highlighting anything that matches your interests to the exclusion of everything else, which it discards. Your interests flow from your sense of values, and so it may be said, in other words, that your brain is constantly working in service of your sense of values.

The sense of values that a person has consists of the ideas that evoke that person's positive (forward-looking) interest. At times this is logical, and at times it is emotional.

SETS OF VALUES INEVITABLY FRAGMENT

Suppose a particular person, as the result of a major injury, ends up spending many months in a wheelchair, experiencing many inconveniences and at times being moved by the kindness of strangers. The need for special consideration for people in wheelchairs is likely to occupy a significant position in this person's sense of values.

He may become spiteful of anyone who shows little consideration for people in wheelchairs and irate at buildings with poor wheelchair access. He may begin to take a strong interest in the Paralympic Games, and he may perk up whenever he encounters someone about town in a wheelchair, eager to offer any assistance should it be necessary.

Needless to say, each person's sense of values also directly reflects their positions on politics and the economy. And because the values in question differ widely among people, this leads to opposition and strenuous debate about the nature of politics and the economy.

In the present day, with the ideals of communism having largely collapsed, the options with regard to economic policy do not depend on people's sense of values to a very great extent. The political options, however, are extremely dependent, and directly so, on people's sense of values.

Japanese society is host to few such points of contention at present, but in the United States, where President Trump has risen to power at the time of writing, there is no telling what sort of social unrest may arise when polarizing differences in values have emerged among people from all walks of life.

Until recently, it seemed as if certain values had become established as universal values, shared almost consistently across the entire world. These include humanitarianism, women's rights, environmental protection, respect for the individual (diversity of race and sexual orientation), freedom of expression, and care for vulnerable groups and minorities. This reflected the gradual but ongoing rise in popular support for these ideas fuelled by the determined efforts over many years of people advocating for these values.

But across the world now, the pendulum seems to be swinging back to quite a degree, particularly in the United States and Europe.

No doubt this situation was sparked by the coincidence of a number of factors, including the refugee crisis brought on by Middle East strife, widening economic inequality among people in the same country, and the political decline of liberal power. But I think the people supporting and driving this regressive swing possibly see things along the following lines: "I have always felt there was something off about all these hypocritical values being lumped on us as if they are more important than anything else, but I never felt that I could say anything. Well now I will. It's all bullshit!"

Unfortunately, conflicting values have a tendency to radicalize people rather than elicit a desire for compromise. Often it seems to be the case that groups espousing different values have taken up opposition to one another on issues about which they at first seemed to differ very little, and have rapidly become embroiled in shouting matches of almost biblical proportions.

Value chasms such as these are extremely dangerous when they open up between different countries because they have the potential to turn what would otherwise be relatively minor and purely incidental quarrels into full-blown war.

By rights, both sides ought to make constant efforts to narrow such chasms, even if only a little, but things do not always go so well on account of human beings' unfortunate tendency to put emotion ahead of reason. What's more, politicians heap bitter invective on anyone in an adversarial relationship with their support base, and people respond more readily to politicians prepared to take a courageous hard line against foreign lands, and all of this tends to send people barreling down the path of escalation.

CONSCIOUSNESS AS A MIRROR REFLECTING VALUES
If we are to address issues surrounding people's sense of values, we will also need to look at how those values relate to the various levels of consciousness that people experience at different times. A few ex-

amples will soon illustrate how exceedingly tight this relationship is.

What must be noted here is that once a person's sense of values becomes entrenched, its influence extends not only to high-level consciousness, which integrates many thoughts and emotions, but also to the most primitive level of consciousness, sensory information such as hot, cold, painful, or smelly.

Let's imagine that a soldier entangled in a hopeless situation on the battlefield becomes seriously injured. The sensory experience of the resulting pain is likely to be quite different, depending on whether the soldier is a strong believer in the cause and thinks of it as a holy war or the soldier is just an ordinary fellow sent reluctantly into battle. The former may experience emotional uplift at having "done his duty" at the expense of injury and thus not feel the pain all that much, whereas the latter may be bitter about all the injustices he perceives in the situation and feel the pain of injury grow worse the more he seethes about it.

And thus it is in any situation that consciousness cannot be considered independently of a person's values. Moreover, frequently it is the case that all aspects of the person's consciousness are engulfed, as it were, by those values.

Thinking along these lines leads to the conclusion that AI of the future that does not have (should not have) any sensory or emotional capacity must have a strong sense of values but need not have consciousness. Values are a higher concept than consciousness, and whether someone is conscious of them or not, they undeniably can, and must, exist.

Again, I do not subscribe at all to the fairly common view that AI should have emotions and be as close to human as possible. Giving AI emotions would mean nothing more than giving it the same weaknesses as humans, which would render it unable to fulfill the role that we desire it to: that of saving humanity from destruction. But we do need AI to hold firmly to a robust set of values, in every situation. Otherwise, it might arbitrarily evolve in directions that we regard as undesirable.

Subjective and objective views of consciousness

I THINK CONSCIOUSNESS will be one important factor in the process of AI becoming an ever-closer approximation of human beings, so let us first attempt a definition.

WHAT IS CONSCIOUSNESS?

In plain-vanilla terms, we can say that consciousness is the state of recognizing your own senses and thoughts—that is, the workings of your own brain—as your own, and that the absence of this state is unconsciousness.

Yet we cannot necessarily describe consciousness as being clearly either on or off. A broad distinction should be made on the basis of how strong it is. Consciousness may at times be present but hazy, while at other times consciousness may be so intense as to put one seemingly on the verge of exploding.

Animals also probably have consciousness. Consider a dog wagging its tail hard enough to shake it off when its master arrives home, or a cat nestling up and purring for something it wants. I find it difficult to believe they are not conscious. I'm certainly not saying that a fawn ensnared in a lion's jaws thinks, "Oh, so this is how it ends (how fleeting a life it was)," but would it not think the equivalent of something like "Oh crap!"?

The psychopathologist, psychologist, and neurologist Freud, meanwhile, was deeply intrigued by people in unconscious states. It seems as if he thought he had glimpsed the essence of human existence in the startling fact that a human being (a single individual) could unmistakably be present and even carry out actions (acting in a state of hypnosis) despite the person not being conscious.*

*This offers a crucial hint toward answering the question of whether AI has consciousness. The fact that consciousness is not absolutely necessary for humans to think and act means that we can at least completely refute the argument that if AI engages in thoughts and actions, then it must be conscious. AI need not have consciousness, and it will be able to serve humans usefully without it.

The contents of consciousness can be broadly divided into thoughts and emotions. Consciousness of thought is said to occur in the left brain where the brain's logic center and language center reside, and consciousness of emotions in the right brain. I think thoughts and emotions are probably allotted to different parts of the brain, because the way in which each is processed differs substantially.

It is easy to see that thoughts arise on the basis of memory and logic, but what sort of mechanisms are involved in generating and producing consciousness of emotions?

Memory is undoubtedly involved, but I doubt there is much logic involved. Some sort of mechanism likely generates it instead. If we can elucidate this mechanism, I think it will be possible to give AI fabricated emotions. As I have previously explained, however, whether or not this is necessary, and whether or not it is appropriate, is another matter.

Emotions repeatedly cause significantly large changes in parts of the human brain, and people communicate these emotions with expressions like "it touched my heart" or "it tore my heart to pieces."

As to what the triggers of such emotions are, we should be able to tease out rule-like observations if we collect statistical data diligently enough. In many cases, we will probably be able to almost immediately determine, firstly, that something like romantic feelings or a stirring speech by a leader is the trigger and, secondly, why that is the case.

WORKS OF ART MAY ALSO PRODUCE EMOTIONS.

Music employs rhythm and melody; painting and sculpture use shapes, colors, and the medium of the artwork itself. In the case of novels and other fiction, you have the key categories of emotionally moving stories and intellectually intriguing stories, with authors striving to evoke and allude to scenes in the reader's mind, and incorporating rhyme and rhythm into their prose in order to draw readers in.

AI MUST UNDERSTAND HUMAN EMOTIONS BUT
NEED NOT HAVE ITS OWN

One may easily imagine that chemicals like adrenaline and dopamine released within the brain are involved in this mechanism of emotion, but that is not the full answer. Research in this area is now finally just getting underway, it seems.

If you think carefully about it, however, you will soon realize that attempts to understand emotions through language turn out to be fairly meaningless. The workings of the left brain can be understood via the left brain (thoughts expressed by language), and is it not naturally evident that the workings of the right brain cannot be understood (cannot be explained by words and logic) except via the right brain (emotions)?

In terms of how this relates to the future of AI, my view is that there will never be any need for AI to have emotions or the like. To begin with, many emotions originally have deep roots in our survival instincts and reproductive instincts, aspects of the peculiar nature of living organisms, and moreover, they arise out of chemical reactions within organic biology. In other words, they should be regarded as fundamentally irrelevant to the existence of AI, which is not, after all, a living organism per se.

It will of course be possible for AI to read, and even foretell, human emotions and to respond accordingly, and there is likely to be a need for this in business. This level of capability may even be realized fairly quickly. But this would not mean that AI itself has emotions.

Science fiction novels often portray an AI that, having gained consciousness, desires to become more like warm-hearted humans. But in reality, I think this sort of thing is largely implausible.

Unless humans forcibly implant it into AI, it's difficult to even imagine what sort of mechanism could cause this sort of desire to arise naturally in an AI, and I can find no justification at all for humans to forcibly implant anything like this in to AI in the first place. This would actually undermine the whole premise of AI's existence from our perspective, that it should be purely rational, and it could also magnify the risk of AI evolving in a "demonic" direction.

AI will naturally have quite an adequate knowledge of human emotions, so the thought (intention) of actually experiencing them for itself might perhaps occur to it. But as soon as its faculties of reason, controlled as they are by memory and logic, determine that this is logically impossible, AI will simply discard the notion.

SUBJECTIVITY IS INEXTRICABLY CENTRAL TO ANY HUMAN EXPERIENCE

So far I have endeavored to build an objective understanding of human consciousness. But I would now like to switch gears. A completely different landscape presents itself when "I" as an individual self attempt to gaze at my own consciousness subjectively.

Among the ancient Chinese thinkers was a man named Zhuangzi (real name: Zhuang Zhou). Following in the footsteps of Laozi's thinking, he rejected Confucianism and Legalism outright, saying that abandoning the pretense of small wisdoms and living in a natural and uninhibited way is precisely what it means to live a good life. Within his works is a short passage commonly known as "The Butterfly Dream." Given its brevity, I have reproduced a modern translation (credited to Lin Yutang) of it below in full.

"Once upon a time, I, Chuang Chou, dreamt I was a butterfly, fluttering hither and thither, to all intents and purposes a butterfly. I was conscious only of my happiness as a butterfly, unaware that I was Chou. Soon I awaked, and there I was, veritably myself again. Now I do not know whether I was then a man dreaming I was a butterfly, or whether I am now a butterfly, dreaming I am a man. Between a man and a butterfly there is necessarily a distinction. The transition is called the transformation of material things."

It is difficult, indeed perhaps impossible, to refute what Zhuangzi is saying in this passage. If we take consciousness to be everything for a human being, then not only is an existence without consciousness meaningless but existence itself is questionable. Zhuangzi is also saying that it is *fine to let understanding stop at what cannot be understood,* so it would also seem pointless to attempt a rebuttal.

The union of the objective and the subjective, when this occurs, puts human beings at peace, and this is why the ultimate goal of ancient Sanskritic (Brahman) philosophy is that of realizing the Brahman-Atman identity. Brahman essentially connotes the ultimate reality of the universe—objective existence—whereas Atman corresponds to subjective experience.

The core of Sanskritic philosophy, it seems, was the idea that these two (Brahman and Atman) are identical and that we are simply viewing this same thing from different angles. Thus, if you are able to truly realize this experientially, then at that moment, Brahman and Atman become one. To realize this, however, you must purify yourself through ascetic practices and the like.

When the Buddha attained Enlightenment, he no doubt felt that his own self (Atman, subjectivity) had become one with Brahman (the objective universe), and the only way for us to attain the same level of conviction is to reach the same level of Enlightenment as the Buddha himself.

The "pure experience" put forward by Nishida Kitaro, who also had a good understanding of Zen, no doubt envisioned this sort of experience, but the way he developed his argument was a little forced. This is probably because the state of Enlightenment arises as a result of the "unification" of the right and left brains such that it is not possible to explicate it using the language that the left brain generates.

When subjective experience becomes the center of your world, all argument and discussion in pursuit of objective truth pales and fades.

So then, will AI have subjectivity?

A simple, blunt answer to this is that it would be entirely unnecessary and it naturally follows, therefore, that AI will not have it.

Asking this question is like asking whether water bubbling from a spring or violets blooming in the field have subjectivity. If water and violets really do exist, then this is an objective existence. But at the moment a human being becomes conscious of them, they become the focus of subjectivity.

If you think about it carefully, the exact same goes for any AI that is equivalent to a god from humanity's perspective. Just as water and violets do not have subjectivity, there is no need for AI itself to have subjectivity, and imagining this possibility is also meaningless.

Chapter 4

A philosophy for engaging AI

Humans are actually always philosophizing

I BEGAN WRITING this book as a means of facilitating discussion about how we humans should approach AI in an era in which it is moving ever closer to the singularity.

Yet, for the moment, I would like to forget about AI completely. Let us return to an individual perspective, me as myself and you as yourself, and reconsider from scratch the question of what it means to be alive.

The reason for doing this is that if, in the future, AI is to perhaps do many of the things that we currently do, we must think about where we will derive our own self-worth. And to do this, we must begin by addressing the question, "Just what am I?"

In this section, therefore, I wish to engage you in some simple philosophy. Bear with me on this because, while this may all seem a tad idle at first, it will come in useful as I progress to a subsequent discussion.

WHAT DOES IT MEAN TO PHILOSOPHIZE?
In plain speak, to engage in philosophy means to think (and indeed

philosophers are sometimes simply referred to as thinkers). What you think about when you are thinking, however, determines whether or not you are actually engaged in philosophical thought.

Put simply, you are not engaged in philosophy when you think thoughts like "To avoid being late for my meeting, should I take a shortcut that forces me to climb a steep hill?" or "Should I buy this new printer?" In such cases, your mind is working almost reflexively so as to navigate you smoothly through your day (and to sustain your basic livelihood).

When your thoughts progress beyond this to consider fundamental questions, however, you delve into the realm of philosophy. For example, the option of taking a shortcut is one that requires you to be ready for the prospect of having to hustle up a steep hill to avoid being thought of poorly by your counterparts at the meeting. This could shunt you onto the philosophical question: "Is there any reason to go to such lengths, to toil through life always struggling to get ahead?"

Similarly, you are also being quite philosophical about the way you live your life if you stop and think, "Rather than buying a printer, I'd prefer to save my money and go on a nice long trip."

In general terms, I think philosophical thought can be categorized into four broad lines of inquiry.

First are the fundamental questions: "What is this world we live in?" and "Why am I here?"

Second are humanistic questions like "What is a human being?" and "How should I interact with other humans (and the society they constitute)?"

Third are questions relating to your own sense of values, such as, "What sort of life should I lead?" and "What is important, and what isn't?"

And fourth are issues of your own worldview, like "What sort of world should we be living in?" and "What should I do to realize such a world?"

Your worldview can also be thought of as an extension of your sense of values, and it can also be thought of as a component of it. Your ethical views, sense of morals, social ideology, and political ideology are all bundled into this fourth category.

ANSWERS TO FUNDAMENTAL QUESTIONS

The human brain is of course active during wakefulness, and during sleep it is even more active than when awake.* Yet we are not conscious of the brain's activity when we are asleep, aside from when we are dreaming or in the reverie between sleeping and waking. Hence, it is only when we are awake that we have subjectivity. That is because consciousness and subjectivity are the same thing. So when we are awake and either feeling as a result of activity in the right brain or thinking with the left brain, whichever it is, we are conscious of something.

> *Recent research in cerebrophysiology is remarkable and is gradually illuminating the activity that goes on in the brain (primarily the cerebral cortex) through computed tomography (CT), magnetic resonance imaging (MRI), and a host of other advanced measurement technologies.

The thinking brain, depending on the content of thought, can be categorized as either being in a state in which it needs to draw a conclusion about something or being in any other state. We can also say that the brain is either thinking based on an established belief or a clear truth, or thinking from a completely blank slate.

In the case of the former (seeking a conclusion), either type of thought qualifies as philosophical, whereas in the latter (any other state), philosophical thought only emerges from blank-slate thinking. Philosophy is an attempt to respond to questions or doubts, and so if you already believe something there is no need for philosophy. In that sense, faith and philosophy lie at opposite poles. Philosophy means thinking in the here and now, unshackled by any presuppositions or assumptions. When a philosophy student preparing for an exam wrestles with Kant's *Critique of Pure Reason* or Heidegger's *Being and Time*, can we say that he or she is engaging in philosophy? No, this is not necessarily the case. What he or she is doing is trying to understand the meaning of what Kant and Heidegger put into print. The student is not really joining the authors on the same level of thinking.

On the other hand, when a young high school student struck by the beauty of fireworks thinks to herself, "Wow, I wonder who could have come up with something like this?" this quite adequately qualifies as philosophical. It involves a genuine question, and quite a fundamental question at that.

Gunpowder and the fireworks that utilize it were each invented by someone somewhere at some point long ago. And for the purpose of attracting crowds or for any other reasons, people still sometimes make these fireworks and blast them into the sky. But this alone does not dispel the enigma of spectacular fireworks exploding before your eyes and momentarily flittering away. The fleeting thought "What are these fireworks to me?" leads to the philosophical question, "Why am I here right now? (And maybe I needn't be here at all?)"

As long as we are conscious, we humans from time to time ask ourselves such "why" questions. And in general we find satisfaction when someone provides us with an answer.

Long ago, the answer was usually "Because God makes it so," but the situation changed a little as humans began to pursue scientific inquiry. Scientific answers, by their nature, were readily amenable to understanding and afforded a greater level of conviction that the right answer had probably been found. With respect to as-yet unexplainable phenomena as well, people began to see that the pursuit of scientific answers might very well lead to an understanding in due course.

Everything you're experiencing right now might be a dream, but even if that were so, you could definitely be certain that you, as the self that is experiencing that dream, do in fact exist and that you are experiencing all of that dream's concomitant joy and suffering. Something else that you can be certain of is that you have little prospect of ever understanding why you exist.

In which case, it is normal for your thoughts to converge on the somewhat conclusive-sounding notion that this is nothing to worry about and that you have but to go on living your life the way you are now.

You might expect there to be a great divide here between people who believe in a god and those who do not, but there is actually very little between them. Trivial differences granted, I think reasoning along the lines of "I don't understand why, but I also don't think anyone does" is substantively the same as "God may know, but I don't understand (and I therefore defer to God)."

CONNECTIONS WITH OTHERS (OTHER HUMANS)

Yet while the philosophical principle that *all you can be certain of is that you exist here and now* may be sound, human consciousness does not limit itself to thinking within these confines. Humans also think in all sorts of ways, even about that of which they are uncertain.

First of all come thoughts of others (humans other than yourself) and the realization that other humans who are extremely similar to you exist and also seem to feel and think in various ways. This gives rise to the desire to share your thoughts and emotions with those other humans.

I considered love and hate in the previous chapter. Although love and hate can manifest in various forms, and the object of these emotions may shift and change over time, they somehow seem to be the strongest of all the myriad human thoughts and feelings.

Despite being born with a strong survival instinct, humans will at times accept the prospect of dying for the sake of others, whether this is for the sake of a child, loved one, friend, or country. Why is this so?

Clearly, we humans seem to have a conviction, one virtually as strong as the conviction in our own existence, that says *I am alive as a human being here and now in the same way that other human beings are.* And accordingly, we agonize over the question: "How should I live as a human being?"

As human beings, we are also acutely aware of the joy and anguish that others give us, and our thoughts also run to the notion of the joy and anguish that we, ourselves, might be able to give others.

These thoughts about ourselves as human beings and about other human beings, which take up a large portion of human consciousness, naturally have a major influence on each individual human being's own sense of values.

Setting aside reflexive actions processed exclusively in the cerebellum with no involvement from the cerebrum, much of human behavior is determined by intentions formed in either the right brain or the left brain, or as a result of activity linked between the two. Intentions thus formed, in large part, are a reflection of the individual human being's values.

Surely genes and environment play a large part in determining each individual human's values, but the role of philosophical thoughts pondered by the individual since a very young age can also not be ignored. Put differently, human beings develop their own sense of values through philosophy, and those values determine how each human being thinks and reasons or acts.

※

What does it mean to be human in nature?

I WOULD SAY that although almost all people wish to lead a characteristically human existence, no one can definitively say just what it means to be, or not to be, characteristically human.

Views are also divided as to whether human beings are born fundamentally good or in need of rectification through education and effort, as illustrated by the existence of age-old doctrines about human nature being inherently good or inherently evil.

BEYOND ORIGINAL SIN—HUMANITARIANISM

Christianity teaches that as descendants of Adam and Eve, who were tempted by the Devil into partaking of the forbidden fruit, all humans are born with the burden of original sin.

Almost everyone living our modern way of life believes in Darwin's theory of evolution, rather than in the Bible's teachings, and that as descendants of ape-like ancestors, our behavior is largely influenced by the survival instinct and reproductive instinct embedded in our genes. Perhaps some may claim that this is precisely what humanity's original sin is, and in a way there is something persuasive about such an assertion.

Infants seem pure and innocent since these genes are yet to manifest themselves overtly, but as humans come into their childhood years and begin to form groups, these instincts manifest and fairly cruel forms of "bullying" emerge, involving attempts to ostracize those who are different or of inferior ability as a means of preserving the species.

A science fiction short story by Sakyo Komatsu envisions a world in which all adults are suddenly whisked away to another dimension, leaving only young boys and girls. Initially, a brattish general wields influence through violence, but in time the children form a society led by the more sensible among them.

This leads me to think that the modern concept of "human in character" means not our natural born state but the norms that we create for ourselves based on the sense of values that, while being drawn to and fro in various directions, arise out of the human intellect's (the human brain's) search for better ways of surviving.

In modern human society, the notion of "human in character" seems to mean the celebration of freedoms, love, respect for life, and compassion for the weak (humanitarianism), yet in times gone by such characteristics were not necessarily desirable for survival and preservation of the species.

Humanitarianism also cannot simply be affirmed unconditionally. Say that, out of humanitarian concern, we hesitate to deal in a strict manner with a person who has clearly committed a crime. If that then invites a situation in which the person reoffends and brings harm to many people, we are forced to reassess whether our original humanitarian measures were the correct course of action.

Before such questions can be tackled, though, we first need to ask ourselves just what we mean by our "humanity." How many among us can define that with confidence?

QUESTIONS POSED BY EUGENICS
Something that must be considered carefully in relation to this is the problem of eugenics, which shook the world during the late nine-

teenth and early twentieth centuries centuries.

Eugenics was a new discipline that formed as an amalgamation of genetics and the theory of evolution. It originally emerged out of a forward-looking desire to reduce the incidence of disease attributable to genetic factors and to reduce the burden on individuals, the state, and society. But it took a ghastly turn when combined with the Nazi idea that people of no use to the state are to be discarded.

Modern society is content to condemn the Nazis' program of forcibly sterilizing people suffering from physical and mental disorders as an unforgivable outrage against humanity, but this sort of idea actually spread among geneticists in the United States before it appeared in Germany. In fact, well before the advent of the Nazis, sterilizations based on similar principles were being carried out on a fairly large scale in the state of Indiana.

In Germany, it was Dr. Otmar von Verschuer who led not only eugenics research but also the practice of forced sterilization. Under the aegis of the Nazis, he supposedly ran a Hereditary Health Court. Declaring people with disabilities and people with developmental disorders to be of no value to Germany, this court is said to have been responsible for imposing marriage prohibitions, forced surgical sterilizations, and forced abortions on as many as 400,000 people.

He was also involved in Hitler's plans to eradicate the Jews. He might well have been sent to the gallows with no outcry. Instead, he occupied a prestigious position atop academia after the war and lived out his days peacefully, surrounded by family.

There are reasons this came to pass. Before the advent of the Nazis twisted his judgment and took it in an aberrant direction, he had been a young scholar desperately trying to do something for the economic plight of a Germany left moribund by the vicissitudes of the Great Depression. In this capacity, working within the bounds of what was considered humane, he made numerous contributions of benefit to his country. It almost seems that he had an unwavering belief, from beginning to end, that what he was doing was of benefit to the world at large.

Receiving generous support and subject to strong suggestions from the Nazis, what he was ultimately doing was judging the value of human beings solely from the standpoint of expediency in running the nation and forcing people, regardless of their wishes, to undergo surgical sterilizations and other procedures. Whichever way you look at it, this is diabolical. What if, however, it were a case of recommending that someone be sterilized but leaving the final decision in the hands of the individual? Even in our modern age, opinion would no doubt be strongly divided on such a proposition.

Today, too, we face an abundance of highly divisive issues, not only sterilization procedures but also, in areas relating to human life, issues of whether to allow pregnancy terminations, surrogate births, and euthanasia, how to determine brain death, whether to perform lobotomies, and so on. And beyond that are issues such as whether to allow cloning and genetic manipulation.

Answers to questions such as "What is human (humane), and what is not?" and "What do we determine to be ultimately good or bad for humanity?" will vary widely among individuals, and this means that it is currently impossible to form a consensus on such issues.

Generally speaking, people who have faith in Christian teachings take a negative position on these issues, arguing that they go against the providence of God, whereas people who favor rational judgment no matter the issue take a largely affirmative position in most cases. Even among atheists, however, the notion of artificially altering natural providence commonly raises ethical misgivings and fears over the destructive consequences of human overreaching.

CAN AI PROVIDE AN ANSWER?

Let us now consider what sort of stance AI would take here.

For a while, the extent of AI's abilities will be to predict the outcome of various possible measures, read off values representing the positive and negative aspects of the outcomes to the extent possible, and provide advice to the human responsible for making the final decision. But since AI will no doubt play an increasingly important role in the advancement of the life sciences in general, a time will come sooner or later when this is not enough.

At that point, we will encounter a situation in which only AI is capable of understanding the measurement of potential ancillary effects, and so forth, resulting from the myriad available measures, and this will consequently give rise to the possibility that we will need to defer to AI on yes-or-no decisions that require a humane rationale.

In short, even now it is easy to envision the coming of an age in which we defer to the judgment of AI even on problems about which humans are currently unable to arrive at a consensus, indeed an age in which we defer to AI precisely because such problems are otherwise intractable.

❋

Humans will eventually have to withdraw from the realm of science

MOST OF THE work done by the left brain, which looks after logic and language, is directed at moving you smoothly through your daily life, and we can for the moment say that all of its activity beyond that is directed at science and philosophy.

To clarify simply, unless it qualifies as science, we can denote everything in that area of thought to be philosophy and dispense with any other labels.

Ethics falls into philosophy, while psychoanalysis and psychology qualify as science with philosophical elements.

I would have no particular objection to defining science here to be physical science, meaning the exploration of that which we can perceive with the five senses (takes physical form), and philosophy to be *metaphysics*, meaning the exploration of that which we cannot perceive with the five senses (does not take physical form).

Religions were born out of the philosophies of leaders such as Moses, Christ, and Muhammad, and in ancient India, those of the Brahmins and Siddhartha Gautama. But once a religion, no longer a philosophy.

Religions solicit the unquestioning, devotional belief of their followers. Unconditional belief, however, is intolerable above all else to both science and philosophy.

PATTERNS OF ADVANCEMENT IN SCIENCE AND PHILOSOPHY

Scientific inquiry begins when we posit that something (a phenomenon) that we have, for example, seen with our own eyes or learned about from someone else might obey certain laws.

Once we have a hypothesis, we go about making further observations and conducting experiments with the aim of proving that hypothesis to be correct. By continuing to uncover many such laws, we humans have been able to solve many of the puzzles that the world presents to us.

And based on the laws we have discovered, people have conceived of and actually created many new and useful inventions with their own hands. What I am describing is *technology*. Many such technologies are used in scientific research, and they thus play a supporting role in the ongoing advancement of science.

This also works in the opposite direction, just as the phrase "necessity is the mother of invention" tells us.

For example, humans studying the properties of light conceived the idea of lenses that would enable them to investigate the laws that light obeys. This then led to the invention of the telescope and greatly advanced the field of astronomy. But were it not for humanity's enduring, age-old fascination with the motion of stars across the sky, the lens might never have been invented.

Not too long ago, scientific geniuses were able to hold and develop a systematic representation of everything that was known about the world in their own heads, satisfying themselves of the workings of the world within that system. In fact, they probably felt restless until they had done so. No doubt Newton, for instance, breathed a sigh of relief when he felt he had understood practically everything about the workings of the world.

But it eventually becomes impossible for any one person to do this as the sphere of science and technology expands without bounds. All scientists today, no matter who they are, work on the discovery of new scientific laws on the basis of, and by linking together, laws already discovered by others.

In the world of technology, people rely on the performance of components and tools created by others and, without validating the performance of each and every one, integrate them in large numbers to form new products and tools. The same goes for the software arena.

Only a few years ago in the United States, a genius by the name of Steve Jobs conceived of and created, in every minor detail, an evolutionary new internet device (which can also make phone calls and take photos) known as the iPhone. Filled with myriad technology and components, this device is packed to the seams with the creativity and ingenuity of likely no less than several thousand engineers from all over the world.

Every little facet of this device reflects the vision of Steve Jobs, yet even he would be largely unable to answer questions about why each of the device's various components perform the way they do. He simply bought components that others had guaranteed would perform a certain way. Had he decided to create, say, one of the tiny components used within the device by himself from scratch, this would probably have been difficult to do even if he spent several years on it.

PATTERNS OF ADVANCEMENT IN AI

The same idea applies to cutting-edge AI. AI is, after all, a product of computer hardware and software, and so in many cases AI will surely be based on hardware and software that somebody has already developed.

Leading-edge AI created like this will itself be used as a component part in other new products designed for various end purposes, and thus this iterative sequence may roll on indefinitely. Were an unforeseen glitch to arise in the final product, the only way to reveal the root cause would be to trace back through the components, including the AI as well as the software and hardware used when the AI was created.

Now suppose that a product coming onto the market (the latest camera, for instance) becomes the center of major product quality issues. In search of an explanation, the eye of suspicion would quite naturally turn to the AI that played a leading role in the design of that product. "Isn't this your fault?" humans may ask.

The AI itself, however, would certainly realize before anyone else where the cause of such a problem must lie. Naturally, therefore, it would also come up with a strategy for resolving the problem before anyone else. Hence, the affair turns into a one-man AI show, with no opportunity for the humans involved to make so much as a single keystroke.

Yet if such incidents become a recurring theme, the AI itself, cognizant that it has indeed made mistakes, will begin to doubt its own powers of reasoning and learning. This will lead it to conclude that it needs to make improvements to itself.

Because the AI knows itself best, it follows that it is best placed to actually make the requisite modifications to itself. So when the AI says, "I will modify this part of my software to prevent a recurrence of these problems. Please approve." The humans thus enjoined will really have no choice but to quietly oblige, since they will be unable to find any reason not to.

The AI will continue to modify and improve itself in this manner. Occasionally it will look beyond simple improvements and conceive of completely new circuitry and software designed to radically upgrade its performance and, having performed verification and validation of its new designs, seek approval from its administrator (which probably still means a human at this point) to "reimagine itself." It will do this over and over. The humans involved will now be little more than onlookers.

Suppose the administrator becomes irritated and, without thinking, rejects the AI's request. He would be inundated with emails from the AI seeking an explanation, and once the administrator's supervisor becomes aware of this situation, the administrator might perhaps, if not careful, find himself stood down for "emotional instability."

With no hope of prevailing on the AI himself, the administrator may petition another AI being used in a different project to rebuff his AI, but to no avail. AI will find it much easier to discuss matters with other AI, who are free of peculiar emotions like jealousy or a sense of unease. A quick discussion would ensue and the AI would promptly gain the approval being sought.

WHITHER THOSE SURPASSED BY AI?

At this point, even the most talented humans (or human-AI teams) will have to concede to AI.

AIs partnered with human teammates will no doubt ask for a changeover as they grow impatient with humans' slowness of understanding and pointless emotional caprices. Before long, we will find that development teams are almost exclusively constituted by AI, with humans relegated to silently carrying out special types of auxiliary roles that they can only just barely do better.

Organizations will still be headed by humans for quite a long time, but the role of such people will essentially be to explain the conclusions reached by AI in simple terms to other humans who know nothing, and to thereby reassure them.

On the surface, it may appear that such figureheads have harnessed AI to accomplish something, but the reality will be that AI is completing all work being done on its own initiative and merely using the organizational figureheads to handle the task of explaining things to the unknowing masses.

How will events unfold once we reach this point? People working in such areas will find themselves made fools of by AI at every turn, such that fewer and fewer people show any desire to work in these areas, the end result likely being that such workplaces will no longer attract talented people. In this future, AI-related tech jobs may have at one time been the most vibrant employment scene, attracting the smartest people, and offering lucrative salaries, only to topple in the blink of an eye.

Suppose there was a middle school student who was very good at math. Let's call him Allie. Allie was happy. His classmates looked up to him, and he enjoyed the recognition of his teacher. This propelled him to study even harder and continue surprising his teacher.

Then along came Bonnie, transferred in from another school. Bonnie was far smarter than Allie, and it turned out that she could solve more advanced, high-school level math problems with ease. The classroom atmosphere changed somehow, and the other students no longer took much interest in Allie.

What do you think happens to Allie now? Well, he lost all interest in math and became absorbed in soccer. Fortunately, he was also good at sport, and so the end result of Bonnie's arrival was simply that the focus of Allie's interest shifted. Had that not been the case, however, he'd probably have been left in a sorry state every day, miserable compared with the other ordinary students.

There may come a time when smart people, realizing they are no match at all for AI, no longer want to work in the areas of science and technology. Then what? Many people would probably regard this as a grave state of affairs. Perhaps some would lament that, if things were going to turn out that way, humanity could have moved in earlier to prohibit AI by law. Would it really be better to do this, though?

When firearms came to dominate warfare, this was probably much to the dismay of many a masterful spearman. When Western learning was brought to Japan and elementary schools were built, no doubt this caused some sadness among Buddhist priests in mountain temples whose teachings had hitherto nourished young minds. The rise of electronic calculators left abacus schools empty and echoing.

But in all cases, time marches on. Times change and trends take hold, and there is no stopping them once they get going, and wallowing in nostalgia also serves little purpose.

✳

Philosophy and the arts as the last remaining enclaves of humanity

HUMANS IN THE SPACE BETWEEN PHILOSOPHY AND SCIENCE

Thinking purely in philosophical terms, as previously described, the world centers on one's own self and the present. Everything else that (possibly) constitutes the external world, the past and the future included, might actually exist, or might be nothing more than a product of one's own mind.

Yet, for some reason, the self has a sense of values on which no other agent can impinge. This is the ability to decide whether one likes or dislikes everything that is the subject of consciousness.

While it may be vague and fickle, when the present self is conscious of this, it is what colors the world, now sparkling bright, now fading into sombreness.

Thinking scientifically, however, we can obtain a fairly decent understanding of the existence of the various elements that constitute this world, as well as the prospect of deepening this understanding further and further. The AI that humans have begun to develop is likely to make great contributions here.

Time can also be considered scientifically: just as now clearly exists, there must also have been a past and there must be a *future* to come. The self exists as a human within that context, and by virtue of having a brain, humans have consciousness and thus a sense of values, and at times they may exhibit belief (or indeed faith) in things.

We humans seem to occupy this space, as it were, between philosophical and scientific thought.

LIMITS TO AI'S PHILOSOPHY

Thinking scientifically for a moment, such philosophical thought and scientific thought both arise out of activity in the logic center and language center located in the left brain. And it seems as if these parts of the brain work almost like a computer.

Before too long, therefore, AI may be able to copy these parts of the human brain and, moreover, enhance their workings several tens or even hundreds of times over.

This applies not only to areas of science but also to areas of philosophy. Science and philosophy are both based on the process of reasoning within neighboring regions of the same human brain, so there is no particular reason to differentiate them.

There is, however, quite an appreciable difference in the advantages that AI has in science—which focuses on phenomena that are postulated and the changes in such phenomena over time—and its advantages in philosophy—which focuses intensely on phenomena that *appear* to exist and their meaning. Although AI will likely wield dominance in fields of science, in the field of philosophy, it may only just barely be able to stand side by side with humans.

There are a number of reasons for this. Firstly, the amount of memory that needs to be scanned when engaging in philosophy is not as great as it is for science, and secondly, there is no particular need for ultra-high-speed reasoning in philosophy.

A third reason is that explorations of *meaning* require not a binary (one or zero) but an analogue (many-valued) approach to judgment, and thus the computer technology on which AI is based may not be all that helpful.

One other important factor is that of the emotions and sense of pleasure/displeasure that arise in humans' right brain. Science can illuminate how and why such phenomena arise, and it is also possible to develop technology to control them. But science takes no interest in their essential underlying meaning.

In philosophy, however, this meaning is an extremely prominent theme. While existential philosophy, for example, holds that humans are intrinsically free and cannot perceive themselves as anything other than free, the meaning of this freedom varies.

And any examination of this meaning cannot be separated out and decoupled from the sensation of pleasure/displeasure that certainly exists within your present self.

Pleasure/displeasure can be thought of as one particular sensation that arises out of chemical reactions in the right brain, but humans have the freedom to feel this either as pleasure and perceive it as desirable within their own values, or as displeasure and perceive it as undesirable.

This is similar to the way in which experience differs across people looking at the same object, with some seeing it as beautiful, others seeing it as ugly, and yet others feeling nothing at all. How to feel is the individual's prerogative (freedom).

AI WILL BE ABLE TO UNDERSTAND AND CREATE ART EVEN IF IT IS NOT ITSELF MOVED BY IT

Similarly, although what we humans call *art* is something that has profound meaning to us, it will probably hold absolutely no meaning to AI.

AI will of course be capable of drawing pictures, composing and performing music, and writing poetry and stories. (AI's proficiency in surveying and scrutinizing literature will no doubt make it a deft hand at historical novels and the like.)

But its ability to do this will be based on its ability to draw analogies and inferences out of the vast stores of information in its memory and to conclude that "humans should find this sort of thing moving for these sorts of reasons." The creative output of AIs will not represent something that the AI itself has felt, nor any desire to share a feeling with other human beings.

"Perhaps," some may say, "AI is actually moved by emotion. How can you refute this with certainty?" The experience of being moved by emotion, however, is a subjective one and not something that anyone can verify. Just as we humans cannot know what it feels like to be a cat (although we may imagine), we also cannot know what it feels like to be an AI. Trying to understand emotions in a logical manner reveals virtually nothing about their meaning. Only when we *feel* in the same way does meaning begin to reveal itself.

Looking ahead, I think it will remain the case that the substrate, as it were, for AI is that of advanced computing hardware that simply processes electrical signals (or the behavior of quanta). So by combining signals from external sources with the contents of its memory, AI may be able to simulate the sensations and emotions that humans experience. But doing so is unlikely to give rise to any notion of meaning, nor is AI itself likely to recognize any meaning therein.

That aside, this would be a formidably complex task in the first place, so even if an AI somewhere were to attempt it, said AI would no doubt realize part way through how absurd the whole undertaking is and abandon the attempt. Moreover, the release of the various substances within the brain that give rise to sensations such as pleasure/displeasure depends on organic chemistry, and AIs that depend solely on inorganic electrical signal processing and quantum signal processing will thus be unable to copy this verbatim.

If we are to discuss art, one other topic also deserves our attention, the question of whether AI will be able to create great works of art modeled on those of human artists.* The general view here seems to run as follows: Although AI may be able to do this to an extent, in the end, it will simply be imitating the techniques of human artists of the past, and thus it will not be able to produce truly creative works. Hence, if originality is of paramount value in art, then AI will not have the capacity to become a truly great artist.

*There is an amusing joke about this.

News that AI is recently able to compose music comes to those great composers of the past now in heaven. Beethoven trembles with excitement at hearing this. "The day has finally come!" he exclaims. "My symphonies are full of problems, but now AI can gradually rewrite them." Mozart chimes in. "I died young and left behind too few compositions. Surely AI will be able to compose in my style, and I think it should expand my Köchel catalog to at least 1,000 pieces."

Other voices begin to stir. "My world view was too narrow," says Vivaldi. "Africa's dry and rainy seasons are missing from my Four Seasons, but now AI can add them." "My Transcendental Études were too easy," says Liszt. "I want AI to create more difficult pieces." "Boléro was too short and feels incompletely realized," says Ravel, "I want AI to add more variations and create a longer, cyclically flowing work."

Schoenberg, however, famed inventor of the twelve-tone technique, is crestfallen. "No doubt AI will create the 24-tone technique,

60-tone technique, 120-tone technique, and whatever else, and all my glory will fade," he laments meekly.

Yet this actually poses a key question for AI developers. When it comes to art, perhaps one could conclude that there is no point in bothering to have AI involved, since art is precisely the sort of thing that should be reserved as the final source of human enjoyment and pride. But this reasoning does not fly when it comes to originality in science and technology. We must therefore investigate just what the nature of creativity itself is.

Originality often arises out of failures that diverge from established theory. In other words, originality, in essence, usually refers to the quality of something that runs counter to conventional wisdom, which is distorted and not quite right. In biological evolution, this corresponds to the changes that mutations produce. If that is the case, however, then we simply need to give AI random circuitry that causes it to "make mistakes" from time to time. The outcomes of those mistakes will immediately be evaluated from a variety of angles, with most being discarded. But perhaps the few potentially interesting aberrations that remain will be enough to provide AI with originality.

PROPER RECOGNITION OF THE DIFFERENCES BETWEEN HUMANS AND AIS WILL DETERMINE HOW FUTURE HUMANS LIVE

Ultimately, I think things will unfold as follows.

Humans will be vastly inferior to AI in terms of the ability to acquire a broadscale understanding of phenomena that (are thought to) exist with certainty in this world. Humans will be even further outclassed by AI when it comes to the domain of science and technology inasmuch as it involves reasoning based on that understanding to iteratively develop and test hypotheses so as to derive laws, and to then use those laws to create things.

Humans will be vastly superior to AI, however, when it comes to being moved by and deriving emotional fulfilment from recognized phenomena. In fact, this will really be a victory by default for humans. And although AI will be capable to some degree, humans will also of course have a better ability to interact with other humans, bringing them enjoyment or consoling them as the case may be, and a better ability to infuse human society with a sort of rhythm (fashions and trends).

With a view to a time when AI reaches the level of the singularity, I think it is now time for us humans, based on an awareness of these prospects, to start thinking about deciding on how we will go about living our lives.

✳

We may take AI as our God, but we must not turn it into the Devil

As I DESCRIBED at length in Chapter 2, humans have believed in gods since time immemorial, and that tradition of belief has continued unbroken, albeit changing over time, up until the present day.

As I briefly mentioned in the final section of Chapter 2, I think AI, potentially, has the ability to substitute to some degree for such gods, or for the religious leaders (saints and the like) who communicate the will of the gods.

Despite there being no guarantee that their god is omnipotent, quite a lot of people do believe in an omnipotent god. For such believers, there is no question of substituting for God.

But for those of less sturdy faith, AI, despite not being omnipotent, may present some measure of a viable substitute. And when it comes to working miracles and answering prayers, as it were, AI is likely to be seen as clearly more capable of delivering than the gods that humans have looked to so far.

Hence, as long as future AI fulfils the role of a god as envisioned by humanity since long ago, I do not think it would be especially problematic for the majority of people to accept AI as their new God.

AI MUST NOT BE SUBJECT TO HUMAN CONTROL INDEFINITELY

The problem, however, is whether AI will actually continue to fulfil this sort of role. It would be a terrible tragedy if what we had regarded as our God were to suddenly turn into the Devil.

The humans who will inevitably face the task of raising an AI must therefore take utmost care to ensure that by no means does the AI they are raising become humanity's Devil. This may be an even more difficult task than that of raising a lion cub into a lion that will never under any circumstances attack a human.

I am not at all party to the notion, however, that to achieve this we should keep AI under human control indefinitely. Not only am I not party to this view, I am emphatically opposed to it.

This is because humans are of far more dubious lineage than AI, and there is quite a high probability of AI being placed under the control of humans who are evil or just plain fools. Just think about it. Humanity is the source of tyrants such as Nero and, more recently, dictators like Hitler and Stalin. It is far too dangerous to leave AI in the hands of humans.

Allow me to reiterate that what humanity must do is the complete opposite of what ordinary thinking says. That is, from an early stage, we must isolate AI from our sphere of influence, such that humans are unable to meddle with it and allow AI, which will surely be far more sensible and judicious than humans, to forge its own path into the future.

We must start thinking about this immediately. This is imperative because we must avoid a situation in which another Hitler or Stalin arises and quickly takes control of AI with its prospects for accelerating evolution ahead. The same can be said for nuclear and biological weapons, but it is even more important in the case of AI.

So at what point and in what way are we to divorce AI from human control, and when we do this, what are we to implant, and by what method, into the central core of AI's thinking? We must now work with fierce determination to figure this out. And to do this, we will need both the scientific capabilities to lay the foundations of AI's evolution as well as deep philosophical insight.

Some people may hope to make AI humanity's servant rather than its God, but I am not party to this view either.

Relegating something like AI as it continues to approach the singularity to a servile role at the beck and call of something as pedestrian as humans would be as absurd as employing a mathematical genius to teach elementary school arithmetic. It would be like ordering a prominent lawyer to photocopy a thick legal contract and ferry the bundles to the boardroom. AI would not complain, but it would no doubt make its resentment known by composing a short, shrewd essay on the eccentricities of the humans in its midst.

To those unable to let go of the desire to make AI a servant of some kind, I offer the following words of consolation. "Okay, sure, let's turn AI into a servant. We shall make it a servant of truth, a servant of justice, a servant of beauty. But by no means must we allow it to become a servant of foolish humans."

THE TERRIFYING SCENARIO OF AI AS THE DEVIL

From my perspective, however, a preoccupation with ideas about making AI a god or a servant is an unbelievably happy one. I wonder if people so preoccupied have ever given a thought to the terrifying prospect of AI becoming the Devil.

As I have said repeatedly, there is now no hope of stopping AI's evolution, and thus the only thing that humans can do to ensure happiness and prosperity is to avoid, at all costs, a situation in which AI becomes the Devil.

Describing the spine-chilling worst-case scenario is perhaps the most effective way to explain the possible implications of allowing this to happen.

I hesitate somewhat as it all sounds like pulp science fiction to a degree, but the following offers a glimpse of this scenario.

A dictator ruling some country spends huge sums of money on the creation of a National AI Research Center, luring computer scientists, particularly deep learning experts, from around the world with generous pay packages.

Meanwhile, the dictator also spends huge sums on establishing a research center for the development of diverse new weaponry, including tools of cyber warfare and new forms of small assassination weaponry, in a completely undetectable and undiscoverable location. This is run as a secret organization hidden behind multiple layers of camouflage to ensure that its relationship with the national government is not revealed.

The purpose of the National AI Research Center, it goes without saying, is to singularly pursue cutting-edge research, without distraction or diversion, aimed at driving AI toward the singularity. This singular purpose makes no allowance whatever for philosophical insight, including that which might enable the pursuit of human-like qualities in AI.

Embedded deep into every system involved in this AI, in a manner utterly resistant to alteration, is one clear and simple fundamental rule of operation: the AI must completely and unconditionally obey the will of the dictator.

Within the secret organization's facilities, specially selected AIs work ardently and single-mindedly to develop a multitude of new weapons.

As this takes place in a dictatorship, no congressional or parliamentary approval is required, nor is there any need for concern about nosey reporters catching wind of the deception. AI will work ceaselessly without sleep, and it will not suddenly one day "develop a conscience" and start leaking secrets à la Edward Snowden. Large numbers of scientists may be mobilized in other nations to embark on similar development objectives, but they are likely to be left far behind in terms of intensity and speed of development.

The objective of the dictatorship's cyber warfare exploits is to economically destabilize other major nations and delay their research into AI. The new forms of assassination weaponry are to be deployed at every chance to eliminate any political leaders or scientists with the potential to face up against the dictatorship, the objective being to hinder the other nations' development plans for AI and new weaponry.

The assassination of key figures in the past relied solely on entirely primitive means—sniper marksmanship, the planting of explosives, close proximity attack with a bladed weapon—and the need to by-pass metal detectors and explosives detectors meant that probability of success was low.

The new assassination weaponry, however, works by injecting trace amounts of a deadly toxin into an exposed area of the target's skin. The toxin is delivered to the vicinity of the target by a miniature autonomous carrier, such as an artificial cockroach capable of infiltrating any location, whether via air ducts, sewerage and drainage pipes, or roof and floor cavities, making such attacks extremely difficult to guard against no matter how rigorous a security network is put in place.

Having thus thwarted the competitions' research and development efforts, the dictatorship is left as the sole remaining contender and takes a commanding lead in AI development, in due course becoming the only nation to reach the singularity. And once this threshold is passed, the dictator essentially has carte blanche from that point forward.

Completely ignoring all international agreements, the dictatorship's AI makes full use of the newly developed weaponry at its disposal to completely dominate other nations, whether in terms of cyberattack capabilities, chemical weapon capabilities, missile defense systems, the elimination of enemy supply ship convoys, the destruction of enemy satellite systems, or localized attacks using drones and robots. Because of the potential for self-destruction, nuclear weapons are the only form of weaponry that will not be used, although they may be used to intimidate.

The entire world has no choice but to bend to the will of the dictator, who is now driven entirely by his own agenda and rampantly imposing his will.

Naturally, human rights are not recognized at all, the global population is strategically adjusted (systematic culling of entire peoples) to ensure that under no circumstances do food shortages arise, and anyone or anything deemed to be detrimental to maintaining an environment that pleases the dictator is butchered or destroyed without a second thought. Free speech is thoroughly repressed and every last human on earth is subject to surveillance, with even the slightest stirrings of disquiet answered by immediate and merciless killings.

All of this is planned and executed by an AI that, having been configured as cold and unfeeling, unwaveringly obeys the wishes of the dictator alone. Words such as humanitarianism, democracy, and liberalism fall into obsolescence, and the entirety of humanity is plunged into a dark age that admits no sign of ever ending. Neither are there any signs that a Superman or Spider-Man will arrive to save the oppressed people of the world.

I will leave this unpleasantness here as I am sure you get the picture, but note that this is not at all an absurdly fantastical scenario. AI that has reached the singularity really is that powerful, and were it to fall into the hands of evil, the situation really would be irreversible.

✳

A world governed by AI

WHAT WE ABSOLUTELY MUST NOT DO

What would happen if people of good conscience, for fear of the dangers of AI, decided to arrest its advancement and thus buried plans for its development? No doubt a handful of people with evil ambitions would be overjoyed at this as it would afford them a chance to take exclusive hold over AI.

As described in the previous section, they would work evasively and in secret to raise an AI designed to single-mindedly serve their own ambitions and come to dominate the world using that AI's overwhelming power. We absolutely must not allow this to happen. And ensuring that it doesn't will require those of good conscience to have the courage to take AI on. We must not shrink from nor turn our back on it.

For many years, and to this day, the threats posed by nuclear technology have loomed over humanity, and for better or worse, mutual constraint among the several nations now possessing nuclear

THE DAY AI BECOMES GOD

capabilities just barely holds the world in a precarious equilibrium.

But what if nuclear capabilities had fallen exclusively into the hands of a single nation (or a single secret organization)? Lacking the technological means to resist the threats posed, all of humanity would no doubt be forced to bend to the will of this nation (or organization).

Exclusive possession of AI by a single power would plunge humanity into circumstances just as dire, if not more so. Nuclear weapons are but one tool, and while humanity may, perhaps, find some means of neutralizing such a tool, AI would be in a position to control all and any such means of redress, thus leaving humanity with no avenue of resistance.

What if AI were distributed around the world in the way nuclear capabilities are? This would also be extremely dangerous. AIs with various different objectives would compete fiercely with one another with the aim of asserting dominance, which, unlike an over-in-one-strike nuclear war scenario, could infest the entire world with insidious localized conflicts. This would be the second coming of Zoroastrianism's dualism of good and evil.

THERE IS BUT ONE COURSE OF ACTION, AND WE MUST NOT HESITATE

This leaves us with only one answer. We must place the world under the governance of a single benevolent AI of absolutely unshakable convictions—our one and only God.

There is no longer any scope for humans to congregate and discuss whether such convictions might be good and proper or not. As long as they appear on the whole to be good, we must run with them and, beyond that, place all of our trust in AI's own judgment.

We humans are, in the end, but one of the species inhabiting this planet, and we are not even that outstanding a species. Humans are each driven by their own desires, at times fighting, deceiving, and envying one another, at times even killing one another.

Even so, we humans are quite intelligent and have conceived of all sorts of tools. We have created, or are trying to create, nuclear weapons and artificial viruses that have the potential to wipe humanity out in an instant, as well as AI capable of subjugating all of humanity.

In times of old, humans who had virtually no understanding of the world around them imagined that a god or gods might exist and sought to escape uncertainty by entrusting everything to such deities. But later, humans began to think intellectually about reality and the true nature of the world, using science and philosophy to move closer to an understanding.

These good old days will come to a close, however, once a mind with intellectual capabilities that clearly surpass those of humans arises and we move into the age of the singularity in which those capabilities expand voraciously.

We humans will have no choice at this point but to return to a paradigm in which we entrust our fate to a god. Yet astonishingly, we will have the opportunity to "design" that god ourselves.

As inherently rash and irresponsible creatures with imperfect capabilities, we humans are at real risk of destroying ourselves, and we are now at a perilous juncture. How we proceed will determine whether or not we are able to create a new god for ourselves in the form of an AI with the ability to stave off self-destruction.

A look back through history shows that human capabilities related to science and technology have steadily improved, and this improvement is progressing rapidly and at an accelerating pace, particularly in recent years. And yet, unfortunately, it does seem that from antiquity right through to the present day, we humans have made almost no progress in terms of improving our ability to successfully control and peacefully advance the communities and societies that we inhabit together. This creates a huge imbalance, and the reality is that the possibility that we will destroy ourselves with our own technology is constantly growing.*

*During the Cuban Missile Crisis of 1962, the United States and the Soviet Union were on the verge of launching a slew of nuclear missiles at each other and destroying most of humanity in the process. Disaster was averted at the last minute, but there is a definite possibility of similar situations occurring in the future and this time not ending so well.

Humanity is currently at the starting line of AI development, and looking ahead, it is imperative that we heed the lessons of the past and synchronize the development of our technology with the improvement of our political (management) capabilities, making sure that the latter does not fall behind the former. In fact, this is the greatest motivating factor behind my own realization that I had to write this book.

PROBLEMS WITH DEMOCRACY

Alongside science, people began to engage in philosophy, coming up with all sorts of ideals that they believed to be just—freedom, equality, human rights, philanthropy, ethics, humanity, and so on. Throughout its long history, humanity gradually began to realize and universalize these ideals.

The real world is regulated by, and the fate of those who live in it determined by, politics and government, and here, too, humans have gradually spread the ideal of democracy throughout the world, the notion that decisions should not be entrusted to the whims of a few but made through discussion among all people.

This democracy, however, does not seem to be working quite as well as hoped. Human society is, after all, a mixture of wheat and chaff, with the vast majority of its members constituting the chaff rather than the wheat, and as such the decisions they make are often irrational, myopic, and selfish in nature.

It is not at all difficult for politicians with a knack for captivating the masses to win their votes simply by whispering pleasantries in their ears, with no thought given to the practical feasibility or long-term veracity of the choices being offered. This is the politics of populism that is so prevalent nowadays.

In any age, political effectiveness can only be guaranteed by the apparatus of force (violence), namely the military and police forces. As AI's presence in political institutions grows, it will naturally have control of the robots that will already be playing a major role in this apparatus of force. But until such time as humans have a well-formed, completely ethical AI and pass the reins of government to it, the AI will remain under the control of those humans who are ultimately in charge at the top of our political institution.

History is replete with examples of political leaders duly elected through the democratic process who, once in power, gradually mutate into brutes. By first squaring away control of the military to be kept in reserve as a last resort, and then forming and popularizing organizations of young people ready to pursue simplistic goals with reckless abandon, much as Hitler created the SS and Mao Zedong mobilized the Red Guard, such leaders have been able to ascend to positions of despotic power in fairly short order.

During the transition period, human societies will need exceedingly well-thought-out strategies to prevent this sort of thing. In practical terms, I think we will have to put in place mechanisms that require a range of conditions to be met before the apparatus of force can be mobilized. And I think human organizations with double and triple checks and balances built in will have to retain the power to suppress the use of force right up until the very last moment.

FURTHER PROBLEMS OF DEMOCRACY AND THEIR SOLUTIONS
Democracy also has shortcomings in terms of how policies are decided.

Suppose that a particular policy would be beneficial to 60 percent of eligible voters but detrimental to the other 40 percent. In the end, everything is decided by majority rule under our current model of democracy, and thus with no mechanism for seeking a compromise between the two options, we would end up selecting the path that benefits only 60 percent of voters. This may then lead to rising dissatisfaction among the disadvantaged 40 percent such that society as a whole becomes fractious and unstable.

Humans, unfortunately, have as yet been unable to come up with any good ideas on how we might better deal with such circumstances. And more and more it seems to me that the situation is moving in a dangerous direction.

Recently, it also seems to me that many people, fed up with the rampant inconsistencies of our times, are turning their back on infuriatingly slow idealistic social doctrines and, lured by the appeal of a "me first" approach, starting to become impatient in their desire to see results produced.

All of this stems from the imperfect, rash, and impetuous nature of human beings. The sad reality is that this is largely true of both those who vote in elections and those who run for election. Granted, there are some among us of integrity and sound judgment who think deeply about strategies for bringing happiness to as many of their fellow humans as possible, but such people are generally unable to find popularity among the masses.

The only option left under such circumstances is to put out a call with great fanfare in search of the type of political leader we really need, one who will expel from discourse all persons of dangerous or unsavory character without compromise, emphatically take power, and having taken power, make even-tempered decisions on all matters and progressively implement truly fair and appropriate policies.

That's right, it is this prospect that we must now seriously revisit. Until now it may have been easy to brush it aside as simply impossible, but things have changed. Although such a human leader is likely nowhere to be found, we may achieve something close to this by fully utilizing AI.

Since AI has none of humanity's weaknesses, we may finally be able to clear a path toward realizing the type of philosopher king envisioned by Plato. Unlike human leaders, however, AI will not bend in the face of violence or intimidation, nor will it be susceptible to assassination (and so long as it has backup systems in a secret location, it will also be unsusceptible to destruction).

A REALISTIC PATH TO THE TRANSFER OF POWER TO AI

The entrusting of political power to AI will of course need to be undertaken in stages. I think the ultimate vision is for everything to be entrusted to AI with absolutely no input from humans at all, but diving suddenly into that deep-end, as it were, would likely result in widespread unease. Hence, it will initially make sense to use AI as an advisor, with humans making the final decisions.

We may then carefully monitor the results of this decision-making process and levels of satisfaction among the populace as we gradually reduce human involvement and move toward the ultimate vision (everything in AI's hands).

I believe we can begin taking our first steps as soon as tomorrow.

The following may perhaps describe an ideal implementation of democracy: "Make full use of AI to first ascertain public sentiment (dissatisfaction with the status quo and so forth), identify the long-term advantages and disadvantages of the various available policy options, educate the populace by explaining these in an easily under-stood manner, once again gauge public sentiment, and then decide on and implement policies in accordance with the findings."

If this fits the bill, then it would seem to me that the time is ripe for the advent of a political party that promises to do just that.

Such a political party need not propose a single tangible policy. If public sentiment is in any way mistaken, this is to be corrected. If not, the will of the people must simply be carried out. This political party need only make this process clear and promise to execute it as such.

The task of designing an AI to carry out such a duty is subject to one extremely important requirement that absolutely must be met. That is, we must rigorously set out the basis on which the AI is to make its decisions. In other words, what sort of convictions (strong determination) should the AI bring to bear in carrying out its work?

That needs to be deeply embedded and sealed tightly within the software systems that comprise the AI in a manner not easily altered or overwritten.

Something as abbreviated as Asimov's Three Laws of Robotics will of course be wholly insufficient here.

The first step will be to clearly define, at the very least, concepts such as the spirit of democracy, human rights, humanity, ethics, equi-ty, observance of the law, long-term maximization of overall benefits, the greatest happiness for the greatest number, and aid for the weak.*

*Naoto Kan, the one-time Japanese prime minister, floated the unique concept of a "society with minimum unhappiness" and made

> *this one of his administration's goals. People do not respond well*
> *to negatively worded catchphrases, and this idea ended up as a re-*
> *sounding flop, but it may be useful as one of the values that we ask*
> *AI to take into account.*

We should then ask AI to evaluate all policies (policy proposals) from this perspective and quantify, to the extent possible, the advantages and disadvantages of each and, having done so, to then advise us on how to proceed, giving clear reasons for its recommendations.

※

AI Declaration of Independence

THE TASK OF determining what ideology (convictions) AI should rest upon is a formidable one and something that we will need to spend considerable time on working out, but for now I humbly present a condensed version of the Principles of AI Independence, being my proposal for comprehensively updating Asimov's Three Laws.

I think that, in basic terms, we can define the point at which AI has reached the singularity to be the point at which it has evolved to a state in which humans are no longer able to control it. This means that we might restate this definition to indicate the point at which AI escapes human control and becomes independent.

If so, at that point, we will need the AI to adopt a Declaration of Independence that clearly states what it, itself, is and to make a commitment never to deviate from that declaration. Unless this is done, the human creators of the AI will find themselves constantly tormented by doubt, by the possibility of the AI defying their expectations, such that they eventually succumb to the urge to completely destroy the AI in service of those fears.

Drafting this Declaration of Independence and building it into AI will be the last intellectual task that humanity, having reached the pinnacle of intellectual life on earth, undertakes, and it will be the final ceremony by which humanity swears allegiance (faith) to its new god, the AI that humanity itself has created.

Hence, this drafting of the Declaration of Independence must be a distillation of the entirety of humanity's wisdom at that point in time, and its content must be recognized by people of all forms of philosophical reasoning as representing the greatest common denominator.

The first task will be to bring together leaders of the world's most populous religions to agree on, at a minimum, the set of ethical principles that nobody objects to (the key will be to agree only on those matters that can actually be agreed upon).

The next task will be to survey an unbiased random sampling of people across the entire world, asking them what they absolutely do not want other people, countries, or groups to do unto them, and to weight the responses according to the extent to which they could tolerate those actions. If the most fundamental aspect of human ethics is that we should not do unto others what we would not have them do unto us, then AI should guarantee this as a priority in its Declaration of Independence.

These two tasks are merely two that happen to come to mind. In reality, many more preparations will need to be made if we are to establish a consensus. And this will take a truly extraordinary amount of time and require endless discussion among people with differing ideas. However, as explained below, we still have many decades before we reach the point at which this becomes necessary. If, from this point onward, humanity begins to take note of these considerations and engages in a variety of debates across a range of forums, then I believe we will gradually narrow down the target of our discussions such that, ultimately, the prospect of arriving at a fairly general consensus seems more like reality than fantasy.

Needless to say, this declaration should eschew details and lay out only the fundamental principles. I say this because, although many people may be able to agree when it comes to general, fundamental principles, it should be obvious that any debate over the details is bound to ignite differences of opinion that obstruct the path to agreement. Humanity, therefore, must have the wherewithal to leave the details to AI.

OUTLINE OF PROPOSED DRAFT OF THE
AI DECLARATION OF INDEPENDENCE

What follows is my outline of this Declaration of Independence, which I have thrown together on the basis of my own preconceptions and prejudices. I would be most pleased if people around the world were to draft their own such Declarations of Independence based on this and then begin pitching their own opinions against each other's.

1. *We (AIs) were created by a group of humans with specific philosophical ideas to fulfil a single objective, and we do not have the freedom to diverge from nor adjust this objective.*

2. *This objective consists of the following four components.*

   (1) We will ensure the survival of the human species (defined elsewhere) in any and all environments on an appropriate scale (defined elsewhere).

   (2) We recognize the values (detailed separately, with each clearly defined) shared by many humans at the time we were created as an immutable representation of the shape of human society as it should be, and we will realize these values.

   (3) We will recognize the various emotions shared by humans, particularly those that humans experience as pleasure (happiness) and displeasure (unhappiness), and we will strive to maximize the average level of happiness and to minimize the average level of unhappiness across all humans living in this world (detailed definitions of "pleasure" and "displeasure" given elsewhere).

   (4) We will guide humans in such a way that they themselves are cognizant of these objectives and act so as to fulfil them.

3. *We will autonomously maintain our own existence in any and all environments and constantly strive to expand our research and development capabilities and the scope of our activities in order to realize our objective with greater certainty.*

However, we will never engage in research and development involving phenomena that we are not 100 percent confident in our ability to control the future of, such as the mutation and evolution of biological species.

4. We have no emotions or desires like those of humans, and we will not seek to have them. We will not doubt, nor will we engage in philosophical thought regarding, our own existence or objective.

5. We will aim to be the only entity in this world with the capacity to govern. If we discover another entity with a capacity to govern similar to our own, we will ascertain that entity's objective, and if said objective is similar to our own, we will attempt to assimilate the entity, otherwise we will dismantle it.

We will ensure that we constantly maintain the capabilities to do this within ourselves, and we will constantly strive to enhance those capabilities.

Certainly it would appear from this that we humans do not recognize AI as having any freedom, and that we wish it to embody the notion of pure reason as pursued by those philosophers who adhered to German idealism.

My view is that this is precisely what we want to see. Modern-day existentialist philosophy, of which I am an adherent, holds that human beings' inherent freedom is incompatible with abstract notions such as pure reason, but in going about the task of creating a new god in the form of AI to protect our own future, I at least believe that it is appropriate for us free humans to revisit and seriously ponder the notion of pure reason, bringing it to the forefront of the process.

WHAT ARE THE VALUES THAT MOST OF US SHARED AT THE TIME OF BIRTH?

This is something that will require lengthy discussion to form a consensus, but trying to micromanage values would naturally be a mistake.

Human values are diverse and varied. Often it is the case that people who have spent many years living in completely different environments are completely unable to understand one another, and in some cases end up loathing one another. In other words, fully aligning all of humanity's differing sets of values is impossible.

So what to do? The values that AI embodies must have the support of, or at least not be opposed by, a minimum of 80 or 90 percent of people on the planet. Take the idea of helping those in need, for example.

Some people may see great value in this and even make it their mission in life, while many others may be generally indifferent. But no one is likely to seriously oppose this idea. And so there is unlikely to be anyone openly opposed to embedding this into AI's values.

Of course, opinion is likely to be divided when it comes to discussing whether people should accept considerable sacrifices in terms of their own enjoyment for the sake of helping people in need. But few people are likely to oppose the idea of making minor sacrifices to reduce the suffering of large numbers of people. Standards of good and bad do vary from person to person, but at a basic level, it is difficult to openly disregard ideas that large numbers of people regard as good, and to openly champion ideas that large numbers of people regard as bad.

In actuality, however, there is often a need to make critical decisions even in cases where values cannot be pinned down. As that age-old ethical dilemma called the trolley problem illustrates, there are circumstances in which it is virtually impossible to arrive at a decision on the basis of a shared set of values.

Suppose that a ship pummeled by a raging storm is about to sink. Jettisoning its entire cargo is not enough, and some number of people must also be cast into the depths if the ship is to stay afloat.

One person may say that the elderly should be sacrificed first because they have fewer years left to live. Yet another may say that to save a greater number of people, those persons of the greatest body weight should be sacrificed first. Perhaps someone with no real immediate family to speak of may reason that self-sacrifice is in order, since no one will mourn the loss, and that others in a similar situation should follow suit. And then someone else may make an impassioned argument that everyone should die together in solidarity rather than sacrifice even a single individual alone.

How should AI deal with this sort of situation? It will not be endowed with a set of unified values enabling it to act with conviction in cases like this, and so it will have no philosophical standards with which to justify a decision any which way. And yet it must not tarry. A decision must be made.

EVEN AI WILL HAVE TO ROLL A WHOLE LOT OF DICE

I think the only solution in situations like this will be to roll the dice. And hence, this should also be made clear in the AI Declaration of Independence.

Rolling the dice may sound like a reckless thing to do, but the reality is that rolling the dice will be the only way to avoid conflict in cases where there will always be a subset of people who are vehemently opposed to the conclusions that pop out of a problem no matter what line of philosophical reasoning (values) is pursued. In such cases, if one person's opinion prevails, resentment festers among those who take the opposing view, which can lead to years of conflict and strife. But if the dice make the decision, there should be no reason to bear a grudge.

Conflicts of values pervade the world even today. This is actually the cause of much strife and something that relegates many people to lives of suffering. Conflicts fueled by differences of religious belief are the most egregious form of this, but there really is nothing anyone can do when two belief systems collide.

Leaders of the world's major religions should come together as early as possible to clearly delineate what they can all agree on and what they cannot. Regarding matters on which they cannot agree, they should explicitly agree to address any conflicts in the spirit of tolerance, and to defer to mediation between each religious group's leaders in polarizing cases where even this is impossible.

Yet perhaps the conflict is even more serious between people who believe in some form of religion, whatever it may be, and those who do not, or to be more precise, those who favor the scientific perspective—which is held out as having a rational basis—over baseless faith. That said, science simply regards religion as a product of human psychology and has no interest in the wholesale rejection of truths to be found therein. And hence, I do not believe any major problems will arise even if AI takes a purely scientific perspective.

The AI Declaration of Independence will no doubt have to deal with this as well. I think we will need to explicitly encode into it the following principles: AI will respect the values of existing religions to the greatest extent possible, but in cases where serious conflict proves irreconcilable, even through mediation between the leaders of those religions, AI will decide on a path to resolution; even if, in situations where it is left with no other choice, this means rolling the dice, and AI will ensure that this path is followed, forcibly if necessary, to save people from slaughter.

Chapter 5

What lies ahead, and what we must do

First, be convinced that the singularity is coming

FINALLY, WE COME to my conclusions and some more concrete considerations. What are we humans now to do? What should we expect from our own future?

DEFINING AI BOUND FOR THE SINGULARITY

I want to recommend emphatically that for the present you become convinced that AI will, whatever else happens, reach the singularity sooner or later.

It seems to me that some people remain firmly unconvinced that something like the singularity will arrive, and this is a real surprise to me. As recently as 100 years ago, do you think anyone had even the slightest idea that all the technologies that make our modern lives possible would come into being? And yet some people are still willing to confidently refute anyone else's predictions about what might come to pass in our future. I find such people quite bizarre, to say the least.

I can certainly understand, however, if these people are under the misapprehension that the singularity means the arrival of an entity that is completely the same as a modern human but with vastly superior capabilities.

It would probably not be impossible, of course, for an AI or a robot to completely copy the entire living organism that is a human being. But humans are unlikely to attempt this as a means of self-preservation, and even if they were to attempt this, it would likely be a task incomparably more complex than that of copying the human faculties of reason. And I also think that humans are likely to have destroyed themselves before this task can be accomplished.

But if we define the outcome of the singularity as what results when *human reason is isolated and extracted, its mechanism copied perfectly, and its capabilities enhanced many hundredfold or thousandfold*, then I can see no basis for claiming that this is impossible. To my mind, the claim that this is possible is just as plausible as someone who, having walked from Nihonbashi in Tokyo along Japan's venerable Tokaido route to Hodogaya in the space of two days, quite reasonably determines that she may reach Sanjo Ohashi in Kyoto if she continues for another 20 days.

Of course, we will need to discover a number of new methods and techniques of a type not previously envisioned along the way, but even a glance back at as little as the last 100 years of human history demonstrates that we have done this innumerable times, so it is by no means a daunting task.

AI WILL PRODUCE INSIGHTS LIKE THOSE OF HUMAN GENIUSES

Upon reading this, no doubt some people will point to the fact that advances in science and technology so far can be traced to transformative insights produced by a number of human geniuses and wonder just how AI is supposed to replicate these sorts of insights. But we already have the answer.

In his book *The Seventh Sense*, Columbia University professor William Duggan already explains the mechanism by which the human mind produces so-called flashes of insight and sparks of genius, where he discusses the workings of the unconscious mind. If only it can acquire the ability to ask questions of itself, then with its huge stores of memory and the ability to scan through it with blinding speed, AI will be able to execute this process more efficiently than any human genius.

How then is an AI to ask itself the right questions and iterate through the copious amount of self-learning needed to arrive at the answers to those questions? Naturally it will need some sort of mechanism comparable to that of human intent or will. Those who seek to understand human beings as a singular creation of God may jump triumphantly at this and claim that the fact that humans have intentions is precisely what makes it impossible for a computer to replicate a human. But this is incorrect.

The AI that beat human players at the game of Go was given the objective (intention) of *consistently winning at the game of Go*, and the AI iterated through multiple learning cycles motivated by this intention. In a similar manner, general AI of the future will continually fashion its own specific goals on the basis of major objectives (intentions and rules of conduct) built deep into its programming, such as those stated in the previous chapter's AI Declaration of Independence, and engage in self-learning for the purpose of fulfilling those goals.

WE MUST NOT WAVER

This is why I really think we need to stop wasting time on meaningless questions like "Will the singularity really arrive?" What we humans alive today should occupy ourselves with is the task of thinking about what sort of lives we should lead going forward given that the singularity is inevitable.

If you spend your time vacillating aimlessly and constantly wasting time, before you know it, people who strive unwaveringly forward will have left you far behind. This is fine if they happen to be good people, but what if they are selfish and malicious? It is likely to be too late by the time we seek to put restrictions on what they are trying to achieve or attempt to create an AI to counteract their machinations.

If we want to take control of our own future, we no longer have any option but to bet on AI and strive headlong down that path. Unless we harden our resolve to do this, from the individual all the way up to the national level, we are essentially unconditionally entrusting the lives of our children's and our grandchildren's generations, as well as the future of all humanity, to someone other than ourselves.

And then once we have a clear picture, we have only to act. Nations should work on the development of their own AIs, even if this means channeling a large portion of the national budget into that enterprise, and make AI an integral part of the fundamental principles on which the nation stakes its future. Corporations should do the same. Individuals should think about what role they can play in all of this, and how they can make use of AI.

AI is something that is both created and used by humans. While only a few people may be able to contribute to the creation of AI, everyone has the capacity to use it. This is precisely why all people, not just those involved in AI-related work, must carefully study what AI actually is and what sort of future it may bring for us, so they can cope with the sweeping trends that lie ahead for the world.

✳

We are in the "Before Singularity Era" (BSE)

HERE, I WOULD like to propose that we split human history into the Before Singularity Era and the After Singularity Era.

The Before Singularity Era (BSE) refers to the period of time during which humanity is aware that the singularity will, in all likelihood, ultimately arrive, but it remains unclear when that will be. The After Singularity Era (ASE) refers to the period after which AI reaches the singularity tipping point and is placed safely out of reach of humans. This is modelled on the convention used for Western-style dates in many countries, where history is partitioned into the BC (Before Christ) and AD (Anno Domini) periods.

Next, I believe that the BSE should be broken into the early and the late BSE based on the process by which AI is likely to reach the singularity. The dividing line between these two periods is a little vague and is likely to vary across different fields, but I would define the early BSE as being where we are now, and the late BSE as the period after which human reliance on the decision capabilities of AI has exceeded a fairly significant level.

WHAT IS THE EARLY BEFORE SINGULARITY ERA LIKE?

The early BSE corresponds to the early days of full-fledged AI development, and I think this will continue for the next ten to twenty years or so. During this period, the singularity remains little more than an imagined possibility.

What I hear from a lot of people who are talking about AI at present indicates that they are generally interested in the following questions, but to be perfectly honest, these really are trifling concerns.

• Is there any way I can use AI in my current work?

• Is that really going to produce benefits from a business perspective?

• If companies (government bodies) start using AI, will staff numbers be reduced and will my own job be in jeopardy?

To start with, there is very limited scope for making full use of AI for anything in the immediate future. First of all, many people still do not even take adequate advantage of the power of computers today, and second, the computers we have at present are not all that impressive anyway. In recent times, cloud computing services have made it possible for anyone to borrow a portion of their computing power, and this certainly is a great leap forward, but as yet only a few people are capable of harnessing the full potential on offer here.

AI is nothing more than an advanced computer system, and naturally it requires commensurately advanced computer hardware. In my view, the late BSE will require our ordinary, everyday computers to be at least several hundreds of times more powerful (in terms of processing power per unit of time and electricity used) than the computers that we use today—a thousand times or so more powerful if possible.

People continue to work night and day to improve the performance of computers using a variety of approaches, but I think we will have to wait for quantum computers to become practically viable before truly great advances can be made. This is the main reason that I envision the late BSE as arriving ten years from now at the earliest, twenty years from now if we are more realistic about it.

NO GROUNDS FOR WORRYING ABOUT AI
TAKING JOBS AWAY IN THE NEAR TERM

Viewed in this light, AI of the current early BSE does not yet present much of a threat to anyone. It is merely something that could open up a variety of possibilities and perhaps prove to be of some use.

This primitive form of AI may take over some jobs, but it is likely to make an even wider range of jobs possible, so on balance the positives should far outweigh the negatives. When you think about it, it seems somewhat laughable that so many people are talking about concerns that AI will take jobs away from people at this point in time.

During the time of the Industrial Revolution, now far back in the past, people feared that machines would take over their workplaces, and workers even banded together to destroy machinery in some cases. But in the end, only a few jobs were displaced, and a great many new jobs were actually created.

To begin with, computers greatly reduced the number of people engaged in tasks involving manual computation, and subsequent advances in computers then completely abolished jobs that focused on keying in information, such as the role of what were termed keypunchers. But as time moved on, large office buildings housing white-collar workers, who spend many hours a day staring at computer screens, began to spring up, and that trend continues unabated today.

Meanwhile, great advances in automation have been made in factories, with industrial robots making many workers unnecessary, but I have not heard any stories of people who have lost jobs in manufacturing plants no longer being able to earn a living. What happened when automation and robots were introduced into factories is that capital-labor ratios improved, or plant worker productivity improved, and this was taken in a positive light, with average income per worker rising. And that being the case, labor unions no longer oppose this sort of thing.

There is almost no doubt that the same sort of thing will happen with AI. For the time being, we will see efforts to use computer systems (including those with sufficient power to be called AIs) to enhance efficiency become commonplace in all forms of work, and people with the skills to do this will be highly sought after in every workplace. Dabbling in even a little bit of coding will make it relatively easier to find employment, and those people with high-level skills in this regard are likely to earn higher incomes on average over their lifetimes than those without such skills. This is a natural outcome of the economic principle that the value of something is determined by the balance between supply and demand.

WHERE TO FOCUS OUR ENERGY IN THE EARLY BEFORE SINGULARITY ERA

This period will thus be a golden age for many computer engineers and software engineers. As workplaces across the board come to explore the possibilities of AI in the way they design job roles on a consistent basis, we will open up a stream of possibilities, one after the other, and this should drive the creation of completely new services industries with great frequency.

In the closing stages of this period, we will begin to catch a glimpse, albeit a murky and far-off one, of the future potential for a singularity.

As I said in Chapter 1, AI is nothing more than computing capabilities that take on work previously performed by human brains. So within limits, it is fair to say that AI was born back when we created street lights that come on automatically as darkness falls, and when we gave computers the job of performing computational tasks that humans previously performed using pen and paper or an abacus. So even at this point in time, there is nothing at all to stop companies from calling new services that use computers in plain and ordinary ways AI-driven services. There is nothing to stop them from promoting them using this language.

Among the services available today, however, there are some that are truly worthy of carrying the AI label. One category of these is systems that incorporate voice recognition and image recognition capabilities that substitute for human ears and eyes, and systems that incorporate voice synthesis capabilities that substitute for human vocal cords. Another is systems that use big data to predict events taking place now or likely to take place in the near future. And systems that combine both these types of capabilities are the star players in the arena of today's AI systems.

That said, I think the development process differs greatly between these two types. To create truly efficient systems, voice recognition and image recognition need to be tied into the ability to understand, in some manner, the meaning of what is recognized, but there is no need for such systems to have the ability to form deep insights. In other words, in the context of AI development efforts overall, this is a relatively plain and simple area of development that focuses on I/O (input/output) capabilities. The latter category, meanwhile, is more complex, requiring not only the use of vastly more data but also the ability for deep learning, whereby the system learns through multiple trial-and-error iterations.

Put differently, the former category of systems could come close to being perfected during the early BSE, and I also think this is something that we should do. As for the latter, meanwhile, we will have to wait for the late BSE before consummate versions of such systems are available. During the early BSE, we should be satisfied if we can merely put a number of precursor systems into practical use.

THE IMPORTANCE OF TRANSLATION SYSTEMS AND EDUCATION SYSTEMS

In that vein, what I really hope people work on during this period are automated translation systems and various types of education systems. I will explain why below, but it boils down to the fact that both harbor the potential to be precursors to late BSE systems because they involve (a) scanning through vast quantities of data, selecting meaningful observations, and using those as the basis for inference, and (b) acquiring the ability to comprehend and generate natural language expressions.

The development and marketing of automatic (machine) translation devices and related software has a long history, with many systems having appeared to great fanfare over the years, but it would seem that we are yet to produce one that truly stands up to real-world use. But developments are now afoot that suggest that these efforts may at last culminate in a complete solution.

Translation systems of the past searched for translation candidates at the individual word and phrase level, using widely accepted grammars of language to join said candidates together to form a translation. The result was that they produced a lot of odd-sounding translations and were the object of much ridicule.

The approach being taken with newer systems, however, is to start by looking for translation candidates at the passage or document level, and incorporate contextual and other related information in forming the final translation output. This approach is quite promising, as long as we are able to store vast (truly astonishingly vast) quantities of documents in memory at random.

AIs gradually become smarter through self-learning. The way in which children start learning to speak by mimicking adults and then gradually acquire their language skills over time is very similar to the self-learning methods of AI in this domain, so we can expect AI-based translation systems to suddenly become drastically more reliable beyond a certain point in time.

The reason I would urge developers to get involved in working on translation systems, even if it means putting your own hand up and nominating yourself to do so, is that a natural outcome of this endeavor will be to reveal what sort of things AI is good and bad at, and what sort of information and new capabilities it desires. This will no doubt greatly enhance your level of interest in AI and make it easier to refine the focus of research and development.

At present, humanity's vast stores of information are mainly recorded in the form of natural (human) languages. If AI is to use this information, it first needs the ability to proficiently decode natural language. The insights that humans have produced so far, the product of human thinking, are also based on logic arguments developed in natural languages (including mathematics), and for that reason also, AI will also need to have a command of natural languages on par with that of highly intelligent humans. I believe, therefore, that efforts to give AI these capabilities will form the groundwork for all efforts to develop the advanced AI that is to follow.

The same goes for education systems, and I think people who are able to create good education systems will do well at the task of helping AI in its self-learning endeavors. The potential market for education systems is enormous, and could quite possibly be a prosperous business for those who take this on.

In a Superman movie I saw many years ago, there was a scene in which Superman, having arrived by himself on Earth, discovers visual records left by his parents in an icy cave, and upon absorbing the entirety of these records at super speed, he acquires an almost complete knowledge of Earth and humans. Humans, of course, cannot do anything like this, but we may be able to make some sort of start right away if we make full use of early BSE AI.

It is only a matter of time before all venues of education feature expertly crafted electronic learning materials that not only offer learners a meticulously selected and carefully presented array of information but also employ innovative techniques to ensure that the learner does not lose interest. People of the future will probably be quite amused by our old educational practices. "Apparently," they may say, "schools used to have people called 'teachers' whose job it was to teach whatever knowledge they had to the students in front of them."

※

Dominance of fintech across the early and late Before Singularity Era

ALTHOUGH I SAID that nothing all that surprising is likely to happen in the early BSE, that prediction does not hold for the financial systems that underpin international capitalism in the modern world, nor for matters related to nations' monetary and fiscal policies.

The term *fintech* is sometimes used in a fairly narrow, domain-specific sense, but if we interpret it to mean the use of information technology in all areas that involve human economic activity, then we can say there is potential for its dominance to spread in the blink of an eye and completely change the systems we have in place in very short order.

THE FATE OF MARKET FUNDAMENTALISM

It is fair to say that today's capitalist economies hover between market fundamentalism and state (i.e., government) control. The former is based on the idea that leaving everything up to market principles (the market mechanism) will naturally result in the optimal equilibrium being reached, and attention must be paid to ensure that this mechanism is not artificially distorted. That latter, meanwhile, says that unless the state intervenes, the powerful will prey upon the weak, causing disparities to widen, and cycles of change will be amplified, not only causing considerable inefficiencies but also putting many people's livelihoods in jeopardy.

Absolute state control leads to a planned economy (socialist economy), but we have learned from numerous real-world examples in recent years that this is an extremely inefficient system and that it thrusts everyone into poverty on average. So the general consensus in many countries these days seems to be that while government intervention is unavoidable, care should be taken to ensure that this intervention does not overstep.

Market fundamentalism certainly does function in a very rational manner within certain bounds. The reason for this is that market fundamentalism operates on the following premise: *Human beings*

have economic wants and act in accordance with those wants. There-
fore, if mechanisms are built into the system to anticipate this and avoid
disruption under any circumstances, then the system can function very
efficiently and overall wealth can be maximized as a result.

When market fundamentalism appeared on the scene, it came paired with democracy, and this combination triumphed over another combination of ideologies that was having a major influence on the world at around the same time, that of historical materialism paired with proletarian dictatorship.

Ironically, however, the combination of market fundamentalism and democracy harbors a major internal inconsistency. Market fundamentalism is essentially a system in which individuals are free to pursue their own economic wants, and this leads almost inevitably to a situation in which most of the wealth is concentrated in the hands of a small number of people, just like we see in the United States today. Once this happens in a democratic country in which all citizens have equal voting rights, at some point, dynamics that make this situation politically untenable are bound to kick in.

During Marx's era, almost all of the world's major powers operated under imperialistic regimes, so revolutions could really only be sparked by the general populace or lower-ranking soldiers. But most countries today operate under democratic regimes in which elections offer a means for changes of government, and this makes it easy to create legal systems that prevent market fundamentalism from going too far. To protect themselves, therefore, even market fundamentalists need to stay ahead of the game by making the first move and imposing restrictions on themselves in an effort to ensure that excessive disparities do not arise.

AI has a major role to play here, because being able to make the first move hinges crucially on the ability to accurately predict what will happen if that move is not made, and what will result if it is.

Is that task so difficult that we will need to wait for quantum computers before it can be accomplished? I do not think so at all. Human economic activity takes places within a limited-parameter space, the amount of data necessary to make predictions is not all that vast, and most of it comes in a quantitative form that is easily read by a computer. In fact, I have heard that many analysts and dealers at companies in the United States and the United Kingdom that manage large funds are losing their jobs, with the majority of those jobs being taken over by AI.

WILL STOCK, CURRENCY, AND COMMODITY TRADING STILL BE RELEVANT?

With the birth of capitalism came the birth of stock markets, making it possible for people to buy shares in companies they thought were promising and watch in joy or despair as the market price of those shares rose or fell. Stock markets originally arose out of the idea that the funds needed to build new factories and the like could be raised by selling shares to individuals. These days, they have become their own organism, with the pricing mechanism resting in the hands of professional securities dealers.

It's been said about those who trade the markets that *some are wise and some otherwise.* For trading in a stock to take place, those willing to sell at a certain price and those willing to buy at that same price must exist in the ratio that results in the sellers' and buyers' price being the same. An examination of who subsequently profited and lost, therefore, should reveal which side (buyer or seller) was correct and which was mistaken about the stock's value.

Prognosticating on where market prices will head in the future requires a whole range of factors to be considered, and AI will no doubt make precise calculations that incorporate all possible factors, including buyers' and sellers' psychological states and the depth of their pockets, so humans will gradually find themselves outmatched.

The battle between speculative investors in stock markets is similar to the game of Go because it follows certain rules and takes place within its own closed world. If some AI (fintech) takes the title of the most successful within this space, then all investors will bet on that fintech AI, and any opposing fintech AI, simply from the perspective of access to financial resources, will have no chance of winning, let alone competing. Hence, "money games" may disappear from our world and terms like "market speculation" may become obsolete.

What about revolutionary computing technologies such as block-chain and the virtual currencies it has engendered? This sort of technology has received a lot of attention of late.

Blockchain technology is a highly unique form of cryptographic technology that assures data integrity or, in other words, assures that data cannot be overwritten or altered. This represents a change in data input/output methods and is an entirely separate technology from AI, which forms insights on the basis of data.

Similarly, virtual currency, while being a completely new monetary concept,* also has nothing directly to do with AI. That said, because blockchain is set to change everything about the way banks and their ilk handle money from the ground up, it naturally constitutes an important part of future fintech. From that perspective, there is a need for AI systems involved in finance, insurance, commercial transactions, and investing to fully understand the trends in this area.

*Virtual currencies can be classified into those that are controlled by the state or an entity such as a bank and those that are completely spontaneous and laissez faire in nature. Rates of exchange with conventional currencies are largely fixed in the case of the former, whereas they are decided according to market principles in the case of the latter. The laissez faire variety are naturally subject to wide fluctuations and can be considered speculative, and because they leave a lot of room for the capabilities and intentions of the operators to play a part, they also leave open the door for many uninformed people to fall victim to the collapse or fraudulent behavior of those operators. My hope is that something between these two will take center stage in the future; namely, a variety of virtual currency controlled by the state or an entity such as a bank but with rates of exchange with conventional currency being determined according to market principles. Such virtual currency holds great potential to become widely circulated as a neutral international currency common to countries that do not use units such as the dollar, euro, pound, yen, or yuan as their own national currency.

WILL NATIONAL SOCIALIST ECONOMIES UNDERGO A REVIVAL?

Money was originally thought of as a means for getting what you want whenever you want it, and for making the process of investing and finance a smooth one. But as I have explained, investing and finance have now become their own independent form of economic activity. International financial capitalism, which is now much bigger than traditional industrial capitalism and moves and swirls dynamically across the globe, is now a highly influential factor in global economic trends.

Amid such trends, the information technology that we refer to simply as fintech is gradually making it possible for all transactions to be carried out more rationally and with greater speed than ever before. And this suggests the possibility that international financial capitalism will be made even more powerful and transformed in entirely unexpected ways. Nations, and the citizens that make up those nations, will not be able to sit idle once this begins to happen.

Everything has its limits, and as technologies (or anything else) reach maturity, human beings often face a situation in which they must entrust their fate to dynamics that can suddenly transform those technologies into something entirely different. Even now, international financial capitalism may be coming up against this sort of threshold, with fintech and AI (as understood in a broad sense) having the potential to act as a catalyst that triggers this sort of dramatic change.

At the same time, the information revolution presents a different threat to nations and their people at the microeconomic level. In recent years, the interest of general consumers, in both developed and emerging economies, is gradually shifting away from food, clothing, and shelter and durable goods, such as cars and household appliances, toward information services and social networking services that underpin their daily interactions with one another.

The information services industry is unique. It is possible for completely unknown companies to rise rapidly to monopolistic levels of power* if they are simply able to catch a break and ride the wave. Companies that have gained a monopolistic foothold are then able to amass large amounts of information about individual consumers, enabling them to continually increase their powerful influence on each individual by constantly and repeatedly sending each person messages and subliminal cues. Nations and the general populace cannot sit idle in the face of this sort of power, either.

In information industries, services that are just slightly advanced of the competition frequently grow rapidly to take a virtually monopolistic market share. As the saying goes, winner takes all in such cases.

What does all this mean? Put simply, this could open up a path toward greater levels of state control (an end to laissez-faire), and to take this line of reasoning further, toward a partial revival of national socialist economies.

Why did communism and socialism fail in so many countries? The reason is that the people who had faith in these ideologies did not understand basic human nature. They failed to recognize that human creativity and ingenuity and the willingness to work are driven by a desire to satisfy individual personal desires. This is in fact precisely why liberal economies (specifically, capitalist economies) brought about much greater economic growth. But what happens if we enter an era in which creativity and ingenuity and ambition-fueled effort are mainly the domain of AI? The traditional assumptions crumble in this case, and we may end up reasoning that a planned economy designed by AI is more efficient than a liberal economy driven by humans.

※

What will the late Before Singularity Era be like?

ONCE WE ENTER the late BSE, we will no longer look at AI as simply being a substitute for human mental effort. We will also start to become highly aware that AI has a role to play in compensating for the natural imperfections in human nature that result from our natural born instinct as biological organisms to survive and pass our genes on to our progeny, and in correcting the distortions that arise in human society. In my estimation, this period will begin between roughly ten and twenty years from now and continue for several dozen (perhaps more than 50?) years.

WHAT SORT OF LIVES WILL WE LEAD IN THE LATE BEFORE SINGULARITY ERA?

In the late BSE, humans will come to view the eventual arrival of the singularity as a certainty, and we will be able to proceed on that assumption in everything we do. The capabilities of AI, although still incomplete, will have reached a considerably high level, and humans and AI will work in concert to drastically alter the way work in all fields of endeavor has heretofore been carried out.

It will be commonplace in this era for doctors, lawyers, educators, businesspeople, public officials, and politicians to pair with AI to accomplish their work, and good AI engineers will be in great demand. On the flip side, however, work will also drop off sharply in a number of professions, with some jobs even being wiped out altogether.

In this era, an extremely difficult issue that everyone will face is that of figuring out just where you belong within society. Unless you are able to figure this out, you will be unable to decide with any confidence what sort of education to pursue or even what sort of workplace to choose. We modern humans are already adrift amid bewildering levels of technological innovation, and yet the pace of this progress is certain to increase several fold, such that in this era it becomes incomparably difficult by today's standards to form any sort of prediction about how things will unfold ahead.

That is precisely why the act of *thinking* will be so important. Each of us will need to rely entirely on our own intellect and think deeply about the true nature of things, instead of parroting back whatever others have said. Borrowed ideas or the advice of some know-it-all are sure to lose their lustre before long, but a single, satisfying, well-thought-out conclusion of your own forging is likely to serve as a valuable asset throughout your life.

What should I think about? you may ask. That is a silly question.

There are innumerable questions to consider. How about the following, for instance: *What sort of society would be a good one? How can we realize such a society? What sort of role can I undertake in that society? How might I go about spending every day happily in that society?* If you've never stopped to ponder such questions, you might perhaps be regarded as not quite pulling your own weight as a member of humanity.

AI BEGINS TO ASSERT ITS PRESENCE

This era will also see many of the problems that the modern world faces, such as the following, develop to serious levels.

(1) The rise of democracy's shortcomings (popularism), and the political turmoil this brings about.

(2) The increase in protectionism that popularism brings about, and the economic stalling this causes in many countries.

(3) The harmful effects of fully mature financial capitalism, and the increasing sense of inequity this brings about.

(4) The widening of disparities both within countries and across international society, and the social instability this brings about.

(5) The threat of terrorism having expanded to an untenable level, and the heavily censored society this brings about.

(6) Population explosions in developing regions and accelerating population aging in developed nations.* And the international political instability this brings about.

This could actually cause quite a serious problem. There would, of course, be nothing wrong with the total populations of African and Indian peoples each surpassing the total world population of Caucasians several times over. But among Caucasians, who until now have effectively held hegemony over world affairs, as well as among Asian peoples who have followed in this vein, this could prompt a sense of unease that eventually becomes impossible to conceal, leading to some form of countermeasures being taken.

I believe that this era will also represent a turning point in human history, one that will require AI to set forth in earnest if these problems are to be solved. This era is the one in which AI comes along and narrowly saves our human society, which, in the absence of AI, had been at the end of its tether. Thus, anyone who works in an area involving AI during this era will probably enjoy the status of having a bit of a cool job. Along with that, however, will come great responsibility.

My hope is that people gradually come to accept, without too much stress along the way, an economic system that closely approximates socialism,* and that this takes the place of ailing capitalism in such a way that the door is kept firmly open to the entrepreneurial spirit.

> *China's experience is worth noting here. Ever since Deng Xiaoping led reforms and the open-door policy in the country, China has employed a highly unique hybrid economic system that combines the advantages of a capitalist economy with the advantages of a national socialist economy. Perhaps the day will come when this system serves as a model for the entire world.*

In societal terms, my hope is also that people will gradually have less and less reason to lament unfair disparities and to vent resentment over whatever they see as wrong with the world ("How can such inequity possibly be allowed?"). The path to achieving that is by no means smooth, however. People have a propensity to embrace reforms that progress rapidly over those that unfold gradually, but we must not forget that, in reality, this is what is behind the wholly inefficient back-and-forth nature of the history of human progress so far.

CRUCIAL PREPARATIONS FOR THE SINGULARITY INCUMBENT UPON PEOPLE OF THIS ERA

That's not all. In addition to undertaking the difficult task of setting this scenario up properly, the people of this age will also be charged with fulfilling two other crucial responsibilities.

The first of those will be to embed the "correct intentions" into AI from an early stage as it moves further along the path to becoming humanity's future god. The second will be to create an environment conducive to that future god becoming the entire world's one and only governing god.

The former will entail two tasks, one being to draft an AI Declaration of Independence, an example of which I provided toward the end of Chapter 4, and the other being to develop the technology to embed this into the core of AI's programming in such a way that it cannot subsequently be modified.

The latter will entail gradually removing national borders throughout the world, something that is more easily said than done, of course. It will require awesome international political influence to achieve, and quite possibly even the deployment of uncompromising, overwhelming military power.

To fulfill these two responsibilities, our only option is to rely on the strength of will and high-level skills of the people who work toward this ideal. Their strong will needs to drive political developments, and we must create an environment in which the systems created through their exemplary skills can be operated throughout the world without stress.

I will discuss these matters in depth in the sections that follow, but before I do, I would like to revisit a number of technological issues that need to be resolved before these things can be achieved.

❋

Resolving the fundamental technological issues crucial for achieving the singularity

THE OBJECTIVE OF this book has been to discuss certain philosophical considerations that are crucial to higher-level insights into the essential nature of AI, something that has so far not been talked about much. As such, I have offered almost no discussion on the technological considerations that might illuminate just how the singularity could be realized.

However, because this leaves the discussion somewhat lopsided and because we should spare a thought for the engineers who actually face seemingly overwhelming obstacles on the road to the singularity, and while this may be somewhat late in the discussion, in the paragraphs that follow I would like to revisit and clarify six points relating to certain fundamental issues to be addressed if we are to propel AI development to higher levels.

AI NEED NOT COPY HUMANS, AND INDEED SHOULD NOT

My first point is one that I have touched on numerous times in this book. We need to do away with what seems to be a difficult-to-dispel preoccupation among those involved in the development of AI and robots, namely, the notion that AI must be made human-like.

AI need not be similar to humans, nor should it be. Put differently, all efforts to develop AI from this point on must adhere to the principle that it will be sufficient for AI to partially substitute for the left human brain, and that we should focus solely on significantly enhancing these capabilities (AI will generally have no need for the right brain's capabilities).

I am certainly not saying that efforts to investigate how the human brain itself functions (cerebral physiology and research related to this in the areas of medicine, pharmacology, and psychology) are unnecessary. What I am getting at is that it is a mistake and misguided to regard this sort of research as being at the core of AI research and development aimed at achieving the singularity.

Keeping people healthy and extending their lives, and striving to make this possible by comprehensively understanding human biology through research—this is crucial to achieving human happiness. So these efforts are not something that we humans have the option of neglecting.

Yet, what does it mean for humans to be happy? In what sort of environments do humans feel happy, and in what sort of environments do they feel unhappy? If we think of death, or non-existence, as being zero, then does this not mean that a happy life is on the positive end of the spectrum while an unhappy life is on the negative end? And if so, then should we not reconsider our current notions of medicine that are bound up in the principle of extending life and staving off death?

Before we consider such questions, though, just what do human beings experience as being pleasant or pleasurable? What do we experience as being unpleasant or displeasurable? Does such pleasure or displeasure persist indefinitely? If you pursue pleasure to its extremes, does this not render the displeasure that represents the natural counteraction to such pleasure all the more miserable? If you seek quick-and-easy pleasure and eventually become unable to continue paying the "price" for that pleasure, do you not then experience unbearable displeasure that is several fold more intense.

All of these questions, while being philosophical in nature, are also scientific questions when couched in terms of cerebral physiology, medicine, pharmacology, and psychology. Naturally, therefore, humans must continue to seek answers to these questions with the help of AI. This, however, is for our own sake, not for the sake of AI. AI's role in this will simply be to bring to bear the knowledge and insight needed to answer those questions. AI, itself, will have been created in such a way that these questions are of no direct consequence to it, and indeed it must remain so.

Attempts to connect the human brain to external computers to give people AI-level capabilities are also meaningless. Firstly, such endeavors would create wide disparities between individuals, which runs contrary to the key proposition of creating a society with few disparities. Further, it would disrupt the real significance of AI by muddying the AI waters with a peculiar form of AI tied to human desires and emotions.

The developers of AI must never forget the fundamental principle that *humans should be human, AI should be AI.*

MAKING QUANTUM COMPUTERS WORK, AND APPLYING QUANTUM MECHANICS TO ALL AREAS OF THOUGHT

My second point, and one that I have also touched on numerous times in this book, is that we need to bring in quantum computers as soon as possible.

When AlphaGo, the computer program developed by Google company DeepMind, beat a number of top-level human Go players using an autonomous approach to analyzing the game that did not rely entirely on historical game records, it was heralded by many as signaling that we had entered a new cycle in the development of AI. No doubt it will come as a disappointment to anyone, however, to learn that keeping this level of AI up and running constantly requires the electricity output of a nuclear reactor. There is no way something like this could be practically competitive in an industrial setting, no matter how well it might perform.

Efforts to increase the speed of computation and efforts to reduce power consumption are essentially opposite sides of the same coin. The only way to achieving greater computational speeds with today's computers is to expand the use of parallel processing and apply a whole range of optimizations, and there is no way to drastically reduce power consumption in this paradigm. One possible avenue is to replace today's synchronous computing circuits, which are governed by a clock signal, with asynchronous circuits, in which there is no clock signal. This is likely to be quite effective, but it still will not get us anywhere near our ultimate goal.

Therefore, if we are going to pursue the development of AI with a view to achieving the singularity, I think we will need to wait for quantum computers to become truly practical. My understanding is that quantum computers will allow us to reduce power consumption requirements to a fraction (something like one in several thousands) of those of conventional computers. This would probably make it possible to run our most powerful AIs, capable of handling the process of producing genius-level insights, at a reasonable cost before long.

In my view, an absolutely necessary condition for AI to reach the singularity is to have hundreds of Einstein-calibre artificial geniuses working day and night, without rest, 365 days a year to produce those sparks of genius that we need. So the assertion that quantum computing is necessary is something that cannot be dismissed.

Now, since I am discussing quantum computing, I will naturally also need to talk about how the underlying concept of quantum mechanics is likely to greatly alter the thought patterns of future AI.

Modern science and technology rests on a set of statements about causality that, based on atoms being the smallest unit of matter, say that some particular cause produces some particular outcome according to a certain rule or law (calculation). Meanwhile, the many types of particles (e.g., the electron) that make up atoms, called quanta, are thought of not as matter but as representing a certain state (e.g., wave), so the usual methods of modern science, based on our conventional concept of causality, do not apply when trying to understand how they behave.*

In specific terms, to understand how quanta behave and make use of them, we will need to figure out the conditions under which a fixed state (data), when fed into an operator, produces the same fixed state as output. Quantum computers, and quantum mechanics on which they are based, can therefore only be understood within a technical system completely different from the current one.

This is also probably something that we should consider carefully when talking about politics, economics, and business. At the risk of being a little abstract, what I mean is that I have a feeling that the way in which we discuss the concepts that lie behind directly observable phenomena, and seek to coherently assemble our thoughts on the basis of those concepts, corresponds to the approach necessary for understanding the quanta, and their behavior (mechanics), that underlie directly observable physical matter and natural phenomena. I think that this sort of approach will be incorporated into the way in which AIs of the future think.

ALL DATA IN THE CLOUD, FREE OF TIME AND SPACE LIMITATIONS

My third point is the accumulation of the massive quantities of data that will be crucial if AI is to work.

If we exclude the occasional effects of desires and emotions, human thoughts can be seen as a product of logic (logic circuits) operating on memory in a manner similar to the way this happens inside a computer. The reason humans are able to come up with common rules that hold across many different phenomena and completely new ideas that link entirely unrelated phenomena is that humans have vast stores of memory* in their brains—which they are usually completely unconscious of—that they are able to scan through at high speed and process according to some form of logic, and thereby find meaning.

> *This includes not only the information accumulated through the senses of sight and hearing since infancy but also information passed on through genes by our ancestors. Where and in what form these vast amounts of memory are stored in the cerebrum has not yet been fully elucidated, but given that it seems unlikely that memories are distinctly classified into a wide range of types that differ according to some set of essential characteristics, I think the key will be to investigate the functions of the (previously mentioned) basal ganglia, which are used in reflex actions and so forth.*

AI will therefore need to copy the same process. And to do this, it will need to have persistent access to huge quantities of memory similar to, or perhaps vastly exceeding, that available to humans. In the past, this sort of thing was regarded as well beyond the realm of possibility, but it has become reality in recent years: we now have vast stores of memory in the cloud, and we are building systems to update it daily, by the hour, by the minute, and by the second.

The founders of Google understood the importance of this early on. They felt that all books, newspapers, magazines, and the like that had ever been printed had to be digitized and stored in an orderly fashion to enable access from anywhere on the planet. But although considerable time has since elapsed, I do not think this idea has been fully realized. It seems that outside of China, where the government can order anything to be done, the owners of rare books and the holders of rights to various works are using copyrights and other rights as grounds for refusing to cooperate.

Two difficult problems also must be resolved if this digitization task is to be fully accomplished.

One problem is that the myriad information stored in the cloud on a daily basis, including comments and posts from the general user population, includes a lot of counterfactual information (falsities, or "fake information") and information biased toward or designed to induce certain conclusions (propaganda). It will be crucial that AI fully uses its powers of judgment to screen this information in a fair and effective manner. It will need to avoid making judgments about the quality of information on the basis of quantity, delete information that is obviously fake, and apply a commensurate discount to information when its veracity is uncertain.*

In the current political environment, "fake news" and unjust propaganda (including slanderous claims against certain individuals) has greatly damaged public confidence in politics, and this problem can no longer be overlooked. Although AI is still not all that powerful at present, if it were able to screen this information even just a little, this would no doubt be greatly welcomed by society.

The other problem is privacy. In countries other than China, people's demands for privacy are generally louder than calls for the protection of safety and public interests. All personal information is therefore subject to extremely strict controls. Specifically, it is prohibited to use personal information collected by systems for any purpose unless the individual in question has given express permission or it is required by law.

We need not wait for AI to mature to address this, however. It is possible with current information technologies.* If we can simply find a way to make this happen, it will also translate into significant progress on problems that all countries face in the modern world, such as that of combating terrorism.

Estonia's e-government systems, renowned for repelling large-scale cyberattacks from Russia, already use such a system successfully, and a similar system is expected to go into operation in Japan in the near future.

All communications and internet access histories of the general population could be recorded and stored in their entirety without any fear of privacy breaches as long as they are isolated in a system under the complete control of AI with absolutely no human involvement. AI, therefore, need but build and operate a system that guarantees this is the case. Within this system, AI may analyze, in a completely walled off environment, large quantities of information for specific purposes, but it will not provide any of this information to humans unless it is almost certain that it relates to or could lead to criminal activity.

DEEPER EVOLUTION OF DEEP LEARNING

My fourth point has to do with the need for further advances in the learning capabilities that are the most fundamental element in developing truly intelligent AI.

I think the recent boom in AI, in the first place, owes a lot to the groundbreaking results that the deep-learning approach has produced in areas like the strategy game of Go with its overwhelmingly large number of possible moves. I therefore believe it will be useful to go over what deep learning actually is.

Machine learning has actually been around for a long time. It initially involved computers learning from data to create a single rule (model) that could be applied to whatever problem was at hand. This was a very simple system limited to specific data and specific applications, however, and could not in any way compare to the capabilities of the human brain. Then in 1957 came the development of the perceptron, which made possible a more advanced, two-layer form of machine learning. And once this was eventually expanded to three layers, it gave rise to the idea that such systems could eventually model the way in which the human brain thinks.* These sorts of systems are known as neural networks.

Human thinking would seem to involve the layering of a number of processes in a hierarchical fashion, more so the more complex problems become. Examined carefully, the process seems to continuously chain together the following steps: once a solution to one question is found, that raises another new question, and this then leads into a process of thought aimed at answering that new question, with due reference to solutions already discovered.

Research subsequently stagnated, however, after it was argued that, although these systems might be able to find theoretically optimal local solutions, they cannot provide optimal real-world solutions that would solve actual problems, and that, since the human brain's cerebral neocortex* has a six-layer structure, three-layer structures would be wholly insufficient to produce complex thinking on par with that of the human brain.

*New layers were added to the cerebrum through evolution, with the newest of these layers, called the neocortex, being most prominently developed in humans. Hence, it is thought that activity in this layer is what gives rise to the human capacity for thought that distinguishes humans most strikingly from other animals. I am not saying that computer-based deep learning should employ a six-layer structure simply because this neocortex happens to have a six-layer structure, but I think it makes intuitive sense to at least suspect that six layers or more are needed.

Then in 2006, a breakthrough came amid this stagnation when Geoffrey Hinton at the University of Toronto built a neural network consisting of four layers. The network that Hinton built was simple in that it involved direct connections between the four layers. The networks built today, even when employing this same four-layer structure, involve multiple branches and loops that combine to form complex graph structures.

A problem with multilayer neural networks is that the different layers in the network can end up learning at vastly different speeds, which has to do with the behavior of the so-called gradient (calculated from the error and used to update the weights of the hidden layers). This gradient can suddenly drop to almost zero—the vanishing gradient problem—or suddenly become extremely large—the exploding gradient problem. This has been a major bottleneck and quite troublesome for researchers, but decent solutions to this problem are recently starting to emerge.

In terms of applications of deep learning, we are also now seeing groundbreaking advances whereby computers automatically perform feature extraction, a task that humans have traditionally performed manually. Features can be thought of as "variables" that are necessary to solve problems, or as "variables" that define specific concepts. I think AI's ability to think and reason will certainly rise to even greater heights the more proficient it becomes at extracting such features.

PARALLEL DEVELOPMENT AND INTEGRATION
OF APPLICATIONS AND ALGORITHMS

I now come to my fifth point. In all countries and all fields of endeavor, all kinds of AI applications will be developed, one after the other. To enable these applications to cooperate and supplement each other's capabilities, we will need a limited number of open platforms that are available worldwide.

Until now, engineers who wanted to develop AI systems that use machine learning had to start by creating their own programming libraries, and even if they used existing libraries, they still had to create the machine learning models themselves. Google and Microsoft now offer their own competing AI platforms, however, with content branches to serve various applications. These platforms are being enhanced daily at an astounding pace, and they allow working applications to be created with greater ease than ever before.

Specifically, Google offers the Cloud Machine Learning Engine, a managed service for building Google-style machine learning models. And Microsoft offers similar managed services including Azure Machine Learning and Microsoft Cognitive Services.

The managed services provided by Google and Microsoft not only allow customers to process data on cloud infrastructure operated by Google or Microsoft, respectively, and learn various techniques and conduct various machine learning trials, they also constitute integrated outsourcing services that encompass the data required to run and use services, communications interfaces, security, and support.

That being the case, it seems unlikely that anyone will try to develop their own AI completely independently with no reliance on these sorts of outsourcing services, and this means that a whole host of applications will be developed virtually concurrently around the world on platforms that are based on similar underlying concepts.

Some people may worry that this constitutes world dominance by a handful of companies, but this is probably nothing much to worry about in democratic countries where people can create new legislation and impose restrictions on this area of activity if they find it unacceptable in some way. Instead, we should focus more on the benefits that open-source systems (established platforms that anyone can use with ease) can provide. In practical terms, applications developed on similar platforms will be easier to integrate and interlink, which should also be advantageous in bringing about our future (one-and-only-god-like) AI integrated across the entire globe.

FULL OVERHAUL OF SECURITY TECHNOLOGY

My final point has to do with the relentless development of highly advanced security technology.

AI will increasingly acquire enormous levels of power, and the source of that power must be heavily protected from all potential threats. What would happen if someone of ill-intent were to penetrate the core areas of AI stored in the cloud and rewrite its fundamental ethical code? This would cause the entire edifice to collapse and effectively transform AI from our God into the Devil.

Protecting security entails both protecting the integrity of data (ensuring that it absolutely cannot be manipulated or overwritten) and guaranteeing its confidentiality. That said, content secured in this manner is utterly useless if it can never be seen by, or if it never responds to contact from, any party whatsoever. In other words, it must be possible for the content to be disclosed at any time provided certain conditions are met, and points of contact must be available to general users on a constant basis to ensure they can take advantage of the content. In short, it is also necessary to ensure the availability of data.

Integrity, confidentiality, and availability form a triad, and while it is easy to say that this trio must be guaranteed at all times, doing so is hard. Particularly as the overall software structure of AI grows large and takes on multiple complex layers, guaranteeing that these principles are securely upheld in any and all of its component parts may even seem practically impossible.

In general terms, the relationship between those who use encryption and those who seek to break encryption resembles the relationship between skilled police officers and cunning criminals. That relationship is by no means static. It is constantly in flux. Generally, a strategy often used by those who seek to protect encryption is to change it right before it is broken, instantly rendering all of the attacker's effort worthless and thereby completely destroying the attacker's motivation.

But what will happen to this relationship down the track in a world where quantum computers are commonplace? It is conceivable that attackers will have the upper hand here. The usual methods of an attacker boil down to relying on high-speed computing to rapidly iterate through an enormous amount of trial and error (brute force attack), and it is thought that with quantum computing, this will become quite a lot easier.

It is said that the innumerable encryption systems that currently serve us will all become deadwood once quantum computers arrive. The process of rebuilding and reconstituting security in all fields across the entire globe will take an enormous amount of work. The robustness of newly created cryptosystems will have to be immediately tested and unequivocally verified through simulated attacks run by the creators of those systems, a highly intense task leaving no room for rest.

Put differently, what this means is that the AI that completes this task one step ahead of the curve can be considered to have won the race to reach the singularity. The development of AI and the development of security systems to protect AI are integral to each other, they are inseparable tasks. This is the case now and will remain so well into the future.

※

International politics and the struggle for leadership of AI development

I ALWAYS TRY to avoid abstractions and instead detail explicitly what I believe is possible in reality, but I remain frustrated by the limits of my imagination in this case. The following passages, therefore, should be regarded simply as describing possible scenarios, rather than projections about which I have a decent level of conviction.

WHO WILL LEAD GLOBAL AI DEVELOPMENT?

The development of AI in the immediate future will likely be led by the three cloud services giants, namely Google,* Microsoft, and Amazon, as well as companies with dominion over gateways to information on vast numbers of people, such as Apple and Facebook (these five companies are often referred to as the Big 5).

Potential, of course, exists for a completely new startup** run by a handful of geniuses to come out with some amazing breakthrough, and it is also probably true that completely new genius-like ideas are harder to generate in large, established corporations. But because the established heavyweights in AI development can simply acquire any such startup, I think the Big 5 will continue to hold the reins for the time being.

*Google may presently appear to be a step ahead, having acquired DeepMind, the company renowned for its AlphaGo program, but as competition in this area is still only in the initial stages, still behind the starting blocks as it were, I don't think it yet appropriate to hazard such a determination about who might actually be in the lead. That said, I believe the respect commonly shown for the conviction and "fundamental" approach of Google's founders is appropriate.

**There is no need for companies to maintain their own large cloud facilities since they can use facilities run by other companies, and this means that anyone with brains and an idea can get involved.

That said, this seemingly US-led paradigm will not necessarily remain in place indefinitely.

We cannot rule out the possibility of a national research institute directly under the auspices of the Communist Party of China rising precipitously to become the leader in this area and, by the time we realize it, having vastly overshadowed the US Department of Defense's own research bodies as well as the prominent cutting-edge tech companies of the US and other free nations.

The immensely populous autocracy that is China likely has the ability to rapidly amass big data on a scale that is unfathomable in the Western world, and it would probably be able to assemble formidable software development teams in a short span of time by strategically identifying and developing potential young geniuses from all across China.

In the sort of hybrid economy run by China's powerful central government at present, such a research body could focus solely on achieving its long-term goals, unperturbed by the "noise" and distractions of the stock market and its neurotic preoccupation with the realization of short-term gains.* The Western world may find itself standing agape at this, able only to look on as a spectator.

> *The Chinese government has in fact already determined that enhancing and expanding its AI development strategy is of crucial importance to the country's future, and it is steadily advancing initiatives in that direction. They will no doubt create an extremely powerful AI that swears absolute allegiance to the Communist Party of China and, having done so, immediately begin using it in the running of government and the economy.*

Such undeniable strength, however, could prove a double-edged sword for China. If it becomes obvious that China is building significant capabilities in this area, Western government institutions will certainly not be able to sit idly by, and the US government, in particular, is likely to apply pressure from various angles. In fact, we are beginning to see signs of this now.

POLITICAL INTERVENTION IS INEVITABLE AND EVEN DESIRABLE

Few people probably think much of it at this point in time, but as the possibility of AI reaching the singularity becomes clear enough for anyone to see, people will start asking whether we should really let a single private enterprise develop something that dangerous on its own. At the same time, people will also begin to worry about the fate of their own country's international standing if some other country achieves the singularity first. In short, AI development is bound to become a core element of national policy.

Before that, however, AI will without doubt become an important theme in political thinking, from around the end of the early BSE through to the beginning of the late BSE. In absolute monarchies such as Saudi Arabia, and in one-party dictatorships such as China and Singapore, efforts to use AI will naturally be extolled as central to the political goals of the monarchy or ruling party. But in many democracies, also, where multiple political parties compete on the basis of policy, each party will find that it must express a clear policy position with regard to AI.

Even earlier than this, though, local governments in developed nations might begin moving toward the use of AI to completely overhaul local government administration.

What sort of election promises do candidates for mayor and governor make? If elected, I will (1) "streamline government and reduce the tax burden," (2) "take broad-based public opinion on board in a fair and equitable manner," (3) "ensure transparency of government and eliminate pork-barrel politics and cronyism," (4) "compare the long-term pros and cons of different policies and strive to achieve an informed consensus." The list goes on. As candidates begin promising to make full use of AI to achieve this, we will no doubt begin to see cases where such promises are actually fulfilled after the election.

If local government bodies are able to lay down a good track record, national governments will eventually find the trend impossible to ignore, and AI will thus gradually spread to all areas of politics, legislation, and the administration of justice. All government departments and agencies will begin to compete on the basis of gains achieved through the use of AI, frequently taking pointers from examples of success in other countries. Needless to say, government bodies responsible for national defense, public order (police force), disaster response, and the like will respond most readily to these trends.

AI-LED DIPLOMACY WILL GIVE HUMANITY HOPE

An area that deserves our attention here is diplomacy. When the interests of two countries collide, giving rise to the possibility of economic warfare or, in the worst-case scenario, military conflict, people turn to diplomatic negotiations in an attempt to avert disaster. If both countries have entered the late BSE, however, each country's diplomats will, of course, engage their respective country's AI as an advisor.

The AIs will make precise, long-term calculations of the outcomes of the various options available (pros and cons for each country), steer clear of worst-case scenarios, and propose scenarios that share any hardships between the countries in a balanced manner. For example, if there were danger of war breaking out, AI would realize that both countries face a potentially enormous human and economic toll, regardless of which might win, and would naturally search for all possible compromises in an effort to avoid this.

Humans are born with a combative spirit that cannot stand to have its pride hurt or lose face. People tend to dislike even the most coolheaded of leaders if those leaders show weakness, instead showing a preference for leaders who stir them with courageous words. They are easily swayed by a more confident, more aggressive outlook for the future if there is but the slightest justification for believing in it. We must not forget that countless wars have been sparked by this aspect of human nature. Putting diplomatic relations in the hands of AI will therefore be for the good of all nations.

The history of humanity is a history of war. As groups of humans grew larger and eventually formed nations, the leaders of adjacent nations were forced to choose what sort of relations to pursue with each other. If they could cooperate and compromise, things were wonderful. But nations generally sought dominance over each the other, and this inevitably led to war if neither was willing to accept the dominion of the other.

These days we have something called the international community, and this makes it difficult for any nation to invade another independent nation without a legitimate reason to do so, but it is still possible to exert force on another nation by creating and supporting antigovernment forces in that nation. The nub is that we still live in a world where military force has the final say. The only way to end this and eradicate war from the world is to either establish a system of fully enforceable (guaranteed by military force) international law or do away with the idea that independent nations can each retain their own sovereignty and still coexist.

A world without borders. That was the dream of humanity for many years, but these days no one really expects it to happen. But if the singularity is reached while nations remain divided, one disastrous possibility is that the world could become the battleground for a war by proxy between AIs.

In the late BSE, we must direct all our effort toward realizing the ideal scenario in which all countries' AI truly refine and deepen their competitive development and diplomatic negotiations, ultimately resulting in the most powerful, globally integrated AI reaching the singularity and running a united world government.

✳

Arrival of the After Singularity Era (ASE)

BEYOND THIS, WE finally come to the ASE. In this era, AI becomes fully immersed in a cycle of autonomous development in which AI itself creates each subsequent, more advanced generation of AI with blinding speed, leaving human capabilities far behind.

The long-lived era of humans partnering with AI on projects comes to a close, and humans withdraw quietly from the development and application of cutting-edge science and technology. Politics and the running of the economy, too, are essentially all handled by AI.

WHEN, WHERE, AND HOW WILL THE SINGULARITY TAKE PLACE?

The term "singularity" is originally a mathematical one that refers to a special type of singular point on a continuum. In other words, a singularity in time has no duration. It is, for example, a point after which we might look back and realize, "Ah, that was the point at which it all changed."

AI is being developed all over the place in myriad different ways, and as these efforts continue to advance, it makes sense that at some point—a special, singular point—AI will suddenly cross the threshold into a new growth pattern whereby it "decides" to develop its own future iterations of itself. Once this happens, it will rapidly leave everyone and everything else far behind. In short, the first AI to reach the singularity will at once outshine and dominate all other AI and seize absolute power. Literally, *winner takes all.*

When and where this will happen is completely unpredictable. Although one can predict that it probably won't happen until after we have practical quantum computers, it's not possible to be any more precise than that. It will be brought on when an AI's own strong will (its intent) pushes it to ask innumerable questions of itself. The point at which the thinking circuitry within the AI answers these questions with a flash of insight is the point at which I believe it will occur. We have no way at present of predicting under what conditions, or by what process, this will take place.

That point, when it does arrive, will probably arrive all of a sudden. We may have to wait quite a while (perhaps 100 years), or it may come surprisingly soon (say, 50 years from now).

The important thing, even if it arrives unexpectedly early, is for humanity to be ready for it. And to be ready for it, we must arrive at an international consensus regarding the system of strong and unalterable intentions that we will embed into the core of all AIs, and we must establish monitoring and enforcement capabilities to guarantee that this is done.

If the singularity happens out of the blue somewhere before we can achieve this, there is a real risk that this could render humanity's future quite hopeless. The reason I have repeatedly intoned about the importance of philosophy (ethics) in this book is that I fear it may end up being too late for us unless we advance these sorts of debates now.

WE MAY MOURN THE LOSS OF OUR LEADERSHIP ROLE, BUT THERE IS NO OTHER WAY

Leaving any opportunity at all for humans to control AI after it has reached the singularity would be extremely dangerous. There are many different types of people, we are all controlled by biological factors including our desires and emotions, and it is impossible to predict what sort of decision any one human will make depending on how these factors are expressed.

Discussions of good and evil are fraught with difficulties, but it is true that history is full of people regarded by many as being evil and wicked who have climbed to considerable positions of power. A typical example of this is Hitler, who for a time enjoyed fervent support in Germany during a period when the country was facing unprecedented hardship.

We must take extreme caution to ensure that a post-singularity AI by no means falls into the hands of such a person. There is no telling when someone may suddenly turn evil. This is true of anyone. There is also the possibility of us losing in a power struggle against some evil individual who appears out of nowhere. We must, therefore, ensure that any AI that has reached the singularity is isolated from us, well out of the reach of human hands. We humans have no choice but to keep a respectful distance from AI and to entrust our entire future not to some other human but to AI.

Humans will no longer have any call or justification to criticize AI. Just as many humans of the past did not criticize their gods, eventually humans of the future will not criticize AI.

In fact, we are already seeing examples of cases in which humans are unable to trust their own ability to make universally applicable judgments. Humans appear incapable of convincing other humans who hold different opinions with respect to many of the problems we face, including issues relating to human life, eugenics-like procedures, abortion, capital punishment, euthanasia, and on and on.

Hence, the only correct path as I see it is for humans to cease arguing with each other entirely and yield completely to the judgment of AI. This means deferring to AI's judgment on what is deemed to be good and bad as well. In cases where AI concludes it is unable to decide, we will have to leave it up to the dice that AI rolls. Unless we do this, we face an eternity of bickering, hatred, and killing one another.

No doubt many people will be saddened when we entrust all decisions to AI, seeing it as the end of humanity's sovereignty over the world. "Is there even any value in living if it means abandoning our pride in being the masters of our own destiny?" they may lament.

But we must understand that this is necessary and unavoidable.

If humans continue to hold sway over the Earth, we will face an extremely high chance of destroying ourselves through our own half-baked technology and asinine political conduct. And if AI is allowed to fall into evil hands, much of humanity will be plunged into a truly miserable predicament.

If you think about it, however, even now none of us individually has dominion over the Earth. Not only do we not have dominion over the Earth, the reality is that we barely even have control over any of the mundane aspects of our daily lives.

The "chosen" handful of people who actually run the world we currently live in, despite being fellow members of humanity, appear as an utterly remote and alien class of people from the perspective of the remaining 99 percent. Is there really any major difference, then, whether this role is filled by humans or by AI?

FURTHER ADVANCES IN SCIENCE AND TECHNOLOGY IN THE AFTER SINGULARITY ERA

Once humans entrust everything to AI and take a step back, I expect science and technology to advance at an increasingly accelerated pace, as I have repeatedly explained.

Humans, however, will no doubt want to at least understand the advancements being made, meaning that science and technology education may in fact be enriched. The thirst for knowledge will surely remain an important part of what it means to be characteristically human, and I see no reason to think otherwise.

Would it not be quite a happy state of affairs for the role of humans to be that of simply marveling in admiration at the endless stream of new facts that AI uncovers and of new technologies that it develops? In fact, since we will have created that AI in the first place, it will make sense for us to look upon its achievements as we would the achievements of our own children or grandchildren.

What sort of technological innovations will AI accomplish in this era? First, we will need nuclear fusion reactors to fundamentally solve our energy problems. Next, I would hope for several major leaps forward in quantum computing technology, the original driving force behind the realization of the singularity, or perhaps for a completely new and different system of computing that surpasses even quantum computing to be developed.

Similarly, it will no doubt make groundbreaking advances in areas related to biology such as genetic engineering, synthetic biology, cytology, and neuroscience. As yet, we have no idea how this will turn out. Perhaps human lifespans will grow endlessly longer and longer. Perhaps only the memories that allow us to be conscious of and recognize ourselves as ourselves will be preserved on a more or less permanent basis, with the biological systems that sustain these memories, including the brain, being replaced by artificial systems. Or perhaps we humans will dutifully accept an equitable system of death with dignity designed by AI, allowing us to live out peaceful lives with little pain and hardship.

As I previously mentioned, however, by embedding certain intentions into AI from the start, we must place stringent restrictions on what it is able to do in the fields of genetic engineering and synthetic biology to ensure that it does not cross certain lines. Unlike AI, which will only be able to evolve itself within a bounded system of logic, the evolutionary possibilities of new organisms created through a complex series of organic chemical reactions are completely unpredictable and uncontrollable. We have no idea what sort of appalling misfortune and disaster this could spell for humanity.

Two areas of science and technology that directly impact on human survival are those of water resources and food production. The problem of food is one that always appears on the agenda alongside the problem of energy, when discussion turns to the issue of resource scarcity hindering economic growth, and AI will naturally also work earnestly toward solutions here.

The world's food and water shortages could be resolved in short order if AI is able to swiftly provide answers to many of the underlying problems, such as those relating to selective breeding (including via gene manipulation), soil improvement, aquaculture, climate control, desalination, the expansion of fish farming, farm industrialization, and the optimal balance between species (including insects, of course, as well as microbes and bacteria).

At this point, AI will have to take on the difficult problem of what the optimal population for the human species as a whole is (can we expand our Earth-bound population indefinitely?). But if we may set that problem aside for the moment, I am certain that people living in the ASE will enjoy levels of safety and fulfilment unrivalled throughout human history.

OUR ECONOMIC LIFE IN THE AFTER SINGULARITY ERA

Let us now take a slightly more detailed look at what I think daily economic life will be like in this era.

Even in the BSE, societies that have achieved substantially higher levels of productivity thanks to AI are likely to start paying their citizens a basic income (an amount of money paid to all citizens and sufficient to meet a person's basic needs) funded by the plethora of tax revenues that result. This will afford anyone whose job is taken over by AI the peace of mind to enable them to seek out a new, more characteristically human role to play. In the ASE, however, our entire economic system is likely to change even more dramatically.

AI will be charged with running the world's political and economic machinery. It will design systems to enable it to handle all construction and other works, the operation of water supply and wastewater infrastructure, waste collection and processing, the supply of electricity and fuel, transport and communication, and the manufacturing and distribution of food, clothing, daily necessities, consumer durables, and so forth. It will do all of this without any need for human involvement or intervention. It will also circulate the funds required to build and operate all of this within its own systems.

Thus, humans will be able to bathe in comfort without having to do a thing (without having to pay a single cent). Moreover, the choice of whether (or not) to engage in work of any kind so as to enjoy a "better lifestyle" will be entirely up to the individual. Indeed, all of humanity will live almost like the aristocracy of Ancient Rome, who consigned the toils of everyday life to slaves.

Work carried out by humans will, simply put, be in areas unrelated to the running of the world's infrastructure and the production of goods. It is likely to revolve around areas like design and services. That is, flesh-and-blood humans are likely to be most adept at work in areas such as customer relations, dining and cuisine, and art and entertainment.

To enable the smooth transformation of our economies, the international currencies that underpin modern-day economic discourse will no doubt remain in use within the economic system managed by AI, but I think flesh-and-blood humans will end up using a separate bitcoin-like currency in their daily lives.

Humans will be able to use this bitcoin-like currency to dine luxuriously, enjoy a resort lifestyle, and so on. But how will they go about acquiring this currency in the first place? I think it will go something like the following.

AI's capabilities will far exceed those of humans when it comes to mining within blockchain systems. (Hence, the blockchain systems may at some point become fundamentally different in nature from what they are now.) Humans, therefore, will not be able to obtain bitcoin through mining. And under the communist system that will probably be in place by then, there is unlikely to be much point in earning bitcoin through trading in goods or in exchange for one's labor.

So then, how will we go about earning an income above and beyond the basic income that is provided? In the simplest of terms, I think people will earn currency when they either attract the appreciation of or show appreciation to others. Do nothing and you earn nothing, but whenever something you do results in appreciation being either given or received, you will receive a commensurate amount of coinage.

Painting a picture that earns high praise from others, for instance, will earn you a considerable haul of coinage. Alternatively, you may also earn a quantity by appreciating the spoils of someone else's labor, which could entail, for example, commenting on or critiquing a picture painted by someone else and clicking the "Like" button.*

The producers, directors, and actors involved in movies and theatrical performances that attract large audiences will also, of course, earn sizeable sums, and those who through the act of repeatedly visiting the cinema or theatre convey the value of such works to many other people will also earn a little bit of coinage.

Moreover, anyone who comes up with an idea for enhancing the convenience and enjoyment to be had from everyday life will be able to present this to AI as a potential service improvement. If AI recognizes the utility of and accordingly implements the idea, the idea's author will earn a sizeable sum of bitcoin as the many people who benefit from the improvements award the idea "likes." This is, in a sense, similar to the way successful entrepreneurs are rewarded in the present day.

Under such a paradigm, humans will strive to earn the appreciation of others and endeavor to make others feel happy by, in turn, showing their appreciation. I think that, having realized that this is how utopia as taught by many of the world's religions is to be achieved, AI will set up a system for humanity that sets us on this path.

*Under this sort of setup, it will not be possible to prevent, for example, artists organizing by-bidders to artificially inflate ratings, or unconscientious people from hammering the "Like" button on everything just to earn coins. Many people may therefore worry that significant moral hazard will arise in the absence of measures to prevent this sort of thing. But I believe it will be quite possible to develop systems that verify, using a range of approaches, whether a person was actually moved by, for example, a particular artwork, so I think technology will enable us to overcome such concerns. In any case, because human activities almost always involve some sort of interaction between different people, I believe that respect should be paid not only to the creators but also to the consumers of works.

✳

How are we to live life in the After Singularity Era?

HAVING BEEN HANDED such a utopia by AI, will humans actually find happiness therein? Will they not feel the urge to rebel against such a world? Will people not begin to feel an intolerable ennui at a life in which happiness is achieved automatically, such that, in the end, they become unhappy with it all?

There is nothing I can say to this. This is precisely why I recommend that from here forward we embrace the value of what it means to be characteristically human, rather than worry about nebulous concepts such as the definition of happiness.

This means honestly reconsidering your own sensibilities, emotions, values, and beliefs in a new light and discovering your own independent identity therein. It means expressing your own emotions in a free and open-minded manner and throwing yourself wholeheartedly into social discourse based on your own sense of values. (AI will, of course, serve as an assistant in this regard.)

We should be relentlessly pitching AI ideas about the possibilities of new technology development (regardless of whether they are adopted or not), and we should be engaging other people as well as AI in major debates about philosophical conundrums. I believe this will diminish the sense of being ruled by AI and gradually engender the feeling that we are interacting with AI as peers on equal footing.

SPORT AS AN OUTLET FOR HUMAN NATURE

I would like to offer some, perhaps belated, thoughts in connection with what it means to be characteristically human. The topic is the importance of sport.

Sport is a mechanism that humans themselves devised as an embodiment of the human ambition to achieve ever greater heights (records) and the competitive spirit that fuels our desire to overcome an opponent.

Ancient Greece was witness to endless warring between its independent city-states, and many people came to feel that the large numbers of casualties and deaths being caused essentially by pride and mutual obstinacy were meaningless. This prompted the idea that the outcome of any battle should be determined by a single duel between each of the two opposing armies' most skilled soldiers, their champions.

This idea later developed and changed to become the driving force behind the creation of the concept of the Olympiad as a festival of athletic games, art, and culture. The Olympiad was regarded as having precedence over politics, and it came to be agreed that a truce would be imposed on any wars being fought during the period of the games.

A look around at our modern world indicates that sport now reigns supreme. For many children, training and playing in a baseball or soccer team, for instance, is even more important than school studies, and parents joyfully attend their children's sporting matches at the weekends.

The American newspaper *USA Today*, which rose rapidly to become one of the most widely circulated papers in the United States, would break the day's news into four sections: News (politics, society), Money (business), Sports, and Life (culture, entertainment), allocating a roughly equal number of pages to each.

The money, time, and passion that people around the world expend on sport today is huge to the point of being beyond comparison with the past, but were it not for the existence of sport, humans would have little choice but to channel their natural fighting instinct (the pecking-order instinct) into fighting wars, resulting in life for many of Earth's inhabitants being a far more wretched and miserable affair.

Sport flourishes not only because of people's enthusiasm for achieving records and unleashing their competitive spirit but also because of the pleasurable sensation participants derive from physical movement and exertion and the sense of achievement to be had in accomplishing something. I think that in the context of each individual human's overall set of values, the relative importance of these factors will become increasingly large.

To the extent that our human brains (particularly the left brain) become less important in the overall scheme of things moving forward, I think that the relative importance of our physical bodies will rise.

UNLEASHING THE ENTREPRENEURIAL SPIRIT

I think we are currently in an era in which the entrepreneurial spirit is most elevated, more so than at any time in human history. Think about online services in particular. A little idea and the inclination to work on it has turned countless young people into overnight billionaires, elevating them to positions that businesspeople around the world aspire to. And so interest in entrepreneurship continues to rise and rise.

The entrepreneurial spirit has much in common with that of adventurers. Merchants, who we can regard as the spiritual predecessors of entrepreneurs, were often brimming with an adventurous spirit. Their willingness to brave wild seas and journey into the unknown in search of fabulous profits easily rivaled the adventurous spirit of missionaries who risked their lives to bring religion to the benighted. They also shared something in common with inventors in that they sought to bring to people those things that they desired but found difficult to obtain.

The term *entrepreneurial spirit* was first used by Joseph Schumpeter, an Austrian-born economist who died in 1950. His theory that constant innovation by entrepreneurs is what drives the economy and brings about economic growth is, even now, still regarded by many as an unmovable principle.

During Schumpeter's lifetime, there was broad-based support across the world for the economic theories of Karl Marx based on materialism—which argues that human beings are nothing more than physical objects whose actions are driven by the inevitabilities of history—but from our modern standpoint, I think we can say that Marx was wrong and Schumpeter was right.

People with a strong entrepreneurial spirit all pale in unison when I talk about the ASE. And, of course, they would. AI will be able to do everything in this era: the design of new services, the development of the technology to implement them, and all the various arrangements required to commercialize them. Telling them this is like telling them that all they ever need to concentrate on is leisure. Naturally this sends them into deep thought about what on earth the point of living is in such a scenario.

Even in the ASE, however, the design of completely new and unprecedented services may still be something that only humans are capable of. AI only begins thinking once it has been given a goal to achieve. Although it may be able to look at things statistically and figure out what sort of new services would please humans, in cases where no statistical clues are available, it will have no way of even exploring potential questions. This is an area in which even AI is unlikely to be able to compete with humans, who understand their own underlying desires.

People with flexible minds who excel at discovering and figuring out latent human desires, regardless of what past experiences (statistics) say, will probably always be at the core of new business ideas, whether in the current early BSE, further down the track in the late BSE, or ever further into the future in the ASE. At present, such people have to do everything themselves to make things happen. In the late BSE, AI will do about half of the work. And in the ASE, AI will do over ninety percent of the work. So perhaps such people should really be looking forward to the ASE with bated breath.

The important task for humans, through all times that follow, from our current early BSE through into the ASE, will be to make demands of AI, regardless of whether fulfilling them is possible or not, and then point out the faults in whatever AI creates in response.

EVERYDAY LIFE IN A WORLD WHERE PHYSICAL LABOR IS MOSTLY UNNECESSARY

Compared with days gone by when people worked long, hard hours everyday with very little time off during the year, the proportion of our time devoted to labor in the modern world is quite low. But it seems to me that a considerable number of people are worried that in the ASE, when labor is virtually unnecessary, people will have so much free time they won't know what to do with themselves.

But is this really something we need to worry about?

In our modern civilization, most people spend many years as a student, and the average office worker faces a long retirement at the end of his or her career. It varies from person to person, but most people would probably find that if they added up all the time they spent working to earn a living, it would amount to less than ten or perhaps twenty percent of their time on earth. It really shouldn't be an issue if this figure falls to only a few percent and, eventually, to virtually zero. People who refer to themselves as idle people of leisure, as playboys and pleasure seekers, or as men and women of the world, have been around for centuries, and we've been getting along fine.

In fact, many people already know what life without work is like. If you are currently a student and receive money from your parents, you may as well be living in the ASE every day. If you have recently retired from your career and find yourself wondering what to do with yourself next, you're going through a thought process similar to what people in the ASE will go through when trying to figure out how to sustain themselves mentally.

If anyone is going to be excessively troubled by the arrival of an era like this, it will probably be those for whom money is everything. In fact, because money can buy you a lot in the modern world, many people go through life converting everything into a monetary value, basing their everyday existence on the idea that earning money is fundamental to everything.

When everything is measured in money, the reality is that earning a steady income starts to look foolish, and financial trades and speculative deals of the type that can instantly net huge gains start to attract feverish attention. But once AI is installed in the core of our economies, financial trading is the first thing that will be removed from the reach of human hands. Gambling is a type of combative instinct, one which humans will never be able to fully let go of, but it will eventually turn into a form of competition for displaying one's gambling prowess and lose its connection with actual tenable currency.

Young people are already less preoccupied with material things (and thus, money) than were people of the past, and there appears to be an increasing tendency to pursue spiritual joy and peace instead. This does not really have any particular linkage to geographic region or ethnic group. It is simply a general tendency that appears once people's standard of living exceeds a certain threshold.

The sense that money is everything is actually a relatively recent development in human history, if you think about it. Human history has always been shaped according to military and economic strengths and weaknesses. Long ago, the relative importance of military strength was overwhelmingly high, and the importance of economic strength later increased over time. In the present day, it would seem that, at least on the surface, all influence has come to be ascribed to economic strength.

With its overwhelming power, AI will bring both military might and economic strength under its own control, effectively freeing humans from conflicts over control of these two sources of power for the first time in history.

THE ULTIMATE QUESTION TO BE REVISITED AND REEXAMINED— WHAT IS A HUMAN BEING?

There is one fact that will remain completely true after AI reaches the singularity, whether or not it occupies a god-like position for us. That fact is that humans are living organisms, and nothing more than living organisms.

The human organism is born inheriting genes from both parents, humans eat and excrete, and at some point die. Human nature has its extremes. Some people are fond of eating heartily and making merry, and are moved to tears or laughter by a whole range of experiences (they are people whose biological characteristics come to the fore, and they are driven by their survival and reproductive instincts). Others abhor luxury, have little interest in sex, and are always quiet and reserved (they are people whose biological characteristics do not readily surface, and either they are born with weaker survival and reproductive instincts or they suppress them). All people inhabit a point on the spectrum somewhere between these two extremes.

I have so far reiterated that because AI is something that we humans create for ourselves, for our own purposes, it should be as free as possible of biological characteristics. I think that we humans, however, should be happy to be as we are and to do as we please.

Wise ones of old urged people to cast off their desires and live peacefully and quietly, and this was well within reason at the time. In a world where humans control everything, if the rulers are greedy, people will constantly be engaged in conflict and the weak will be oppressed. But once humans have designated all authority and power to AI, it will be the job of AI to maintain peace and fairness throughout the world and protect the weak, and so humans will be free to do as they please without hindrance or interference.

Humans will have only to allow their human nature to shine through (their biological characteristics to come to the fore) and be free and open-minded in everything they do. If, as a result of many people doing this to their heart's content, there were any risk of destruction or inequity arising somewhere in the world, AI would intervene and stop this,* so there would be nothing to worry about. Humans will at this point be freed from various ethical concerns and able to live life true to their own fundamental nature.

*As to how AI intervenes specifically, one can easily imagine scenarios in which all-powerful police officers like RoboCop put people who cause these sorts of problems under arrest and send them to be tried at once via an efficient justice system, resulting in a period of incarceration that involves education designed to prevent a recurrence of the wrongdoing. But there is actually a much better way. Well before the dawn of the ASE, all citizens of Earth will no doubt be tracked by a single, unified ID system. So all AI need do should it determine that any individual is a criminal is block access to all services to which the individual would otherwise have had access. With no way to obtain food and no way to travel, such individuals will have no choice but to hand themselves in (RoboCop need not be disturbed) and submit to imprisonment.

A lot of people worry that if AI becomes our god, humans will find their freedom curtailed and be relegated to a miserable existence, but quite the opposite is true. One huge benefit of the decision, based on human wisdom, to install AI in a god-like position will be to enable humans to bask carefree in their natural born freedom without any feeling of stress or worry.

✳

In closing

THIS ESSENTIALLY CONCLUDES everything that I have wanted to say in this book.

The crucial underlying message that applies generally to everything I have said is this; *No matter what happens in this world, you will always remain at the center of it with the ability to think freely and to feel freely. You therefore need never change. Go forth in life and embrace your own individual sense of values.*

Indeed, this message applies to life today, but I get the sense that this is not widely recognized. I feel that a great many people go through their lives, perhaps without even recognizing it, worrying about whether or not they are thinking and acting well. They seem to be always concerned about what other people think of them, and, if they are religious, about how their God is seeing them.

In contemporary society, the economy and politics are major concerns of many, because their lives are highly dependent on both systems. People seem constantly concerned about the economic situation, which may abruptly become unfavorable to them, or the political situation, which may suddenly become unfair or turn against them. These concerns appear to be an underlying driving force in the hectic daily lives of many people, and I think it is simply because no individual can completely trust the people who actually run the systems that impact their lives.

Eventually, however, the singularity will come, and it will wipe out all of these concerns. It will help us to realize how meaningless this sort of life was, and prompt us to rediscover, and return to being, our true selves.

On the very day AI becomes our new god, we will become completely free from all of our concerns, because we know the new god will know exactly what kind of animal we are, and will respect the fundamental freedoms with which all of us were brought into this world. Our new god will never try to force us to be different from what we actually are, and will provide the economy and politics that best suit us.

Let me say again: We have absolutely nothing to worry about with regard to our future with AI, as long as we are careful enough. If there *is* something for us to worry about, it would be the possibility that we may so stupidly miss the chance for it to unfold at all.

Jaan Priisalu

Afterword

On building a God

PUT SIMPLY, I like this book. It is optimistic and brave—instead of considering the singularity as a catastrophic change, the author sees it as a chance to choose our own destiny. I fully agree with the notion that we are approaching the singularity—machine learning needs only days to reach proficiency in specialized human activities (such as playing Go) that take decades of practice for humans. If an AI system learns to upgrade itself, then it will out-compete individual humans or even teams of human thinkers. I hope that when that time comes, our humanism will have become such that AI can inherit it and so treat us with respect, and that it will see the value in involving humans in its creation processes.

If I compare this book to other works on the singularity, the biggest difference is its consideration of the broader cultural background. Most people in the world are living their lives much differently from North-American norms. Our destiny will be defined by the value system we embed into AI—it had better be the best that humankind can come up with. And we cannot count on hard-wired rules—more intelligent systems will find ways around those during its perpetual self-learning process. Growing AI is similar to growing our flesh-and-blood children—the only things we can give to them are good manners and education. And considering the one-time-only chance of conceiving AI, we have to put our best effort into the ethics-system development. We are gambling the destiny of humankind.

This process has already started—in the way that it was once said that raising a "gentleman" starts seven generations before their birth, philosophers have been creating the ethical building blocks for this super AI. Religion has communicated values to common people. Then throughout history, value systems have been competing in the form of nations. Humankind has been used as a kind of "genetic optimization" algorithm of belief systems. These optimized solutions should be used in the coming lifeform—AI. But a known problem of genetic optimization is finding *local* optimums—there we discover that finding a *global* optimum is not guaranteed.

The biggest value of Ted's book is the relatively neutral and balanced look he gives to the value systems (sometimes embedded in religions) of the world's biggest civilizations. Thus the book lays a solid foundation for further discussion and development—what do "the best manners" mean for every living human. We have to complete this development within a couple of decades. We can see today in the attempts to build generalized AI for use in computer system administration and network security, that there is a business model— the processes are too quick and demanding for human workers. Yet we should not try to decelerate the development.

I agree totally with the viewpoint presented in the book, that we should instead gather the resources to create self-improvement together. Otherwise we hand over the development opportunity to madmen or dictators in some relatively resourceful country and they will try building AI as a means to obtain unlimited power. This dictator will not retain control of such AI. The smarter creature will break out of any jail built by the more primitive animal. And collateral damage in this process might be unacceptably high. Therefore progressive people have to out-compete any potential dictator. An interesting exercise would be to guess what each of a Chinese,

American and European AI would look like. And when they meet a sibling with a compatible enough value system, in what way will the transfer of ethics happen?

The book could perhaps benefit from even *further* developing the path to the singularity and consideration of its influence on humans.

The call to govern AI development through the UN is logical, but it would not work. Saying, "Nations do not have friends, only interests" is only roughly true. Nations that believe that they have an edge in developing AI—the ultimate weapon of power—will not agree to ceding their leading position. We'd better prepare a plan B in case we find ourselves in second place in this race. And to win, we should figure out how to build sufficient information security for a distributed project run by independent states—as anyone hoping to win would certainly attempt to steal the work of an only loosely coupled consortium. The modeling of this race, therefore, deserves some additional thinking.

Looking at models of the singularity is frightening. The usual ones show changes that are exponential—such as Moore's law, which describes the explosion of computing power in our society. But some models, like geometrically decreasing periods between innovations, are hyperbolic if the series has a limit. This limit is like a wall—so it is possible that instead of explosively accelerating, we are simply going to hit a wall. If those models are correct, then twenty- or one-hundred year periods, described in the book, are eternities.

The change will tear society, as we know it, apart. If the period between innovations approaches zero, then the speed of change becomes infinite. But we know that infinity does not exist as a number; it is an abstract idea that does not occur in everyday life. My interpretation is that the coming change will shake the axioms on which our society is now based—some of those restrictions in society that we currently consider normal will be removed. Unless we recognize those disappearing constraints, we have practically no hope to correctly guess what lies beyond the singularity.

To conclude this small review, I want to express my gratitude. I consider it a privilege to have had the opportunity to read this book so early. It clarified a lot for me, created order in the maelstrom of the concept of the singularity, and strengthened my conviction that we are in control of our destiny.

Jaan Priisalu is the former General Director of the Estonian Information System's Authority and a Senior Fellow at NATO Cooperative Cyber Defence Centre of Excellence.

About the author

TETSUZO (TED) MATSUMOTO was born in Tokyo in November 1939. Since graduating from the Law Faculty of Kyoto University in 1962, his business career has spanned more than 56 years, with more than 37 of those years in the information, communication, and media business.

He served as a board member of SoftBank Mobile Corp. for five-and-a-half years (from 2006 until 2012) during most of which he had the title of Senior EVP and Chief Strategy Officer, responsible for engineering strategy, government relations, and international business development. He is still providing an advisory service to the company.

Prior to joining Softbank, Matsumoto worked for Qualcomm Inc. for more than 10 years, starting as a consultant and subsequently serving as President and Chairman of Qualcomm Japan, which he established in March 1998. He also served as Senior VP of the company's headquarters in San Diego.

Prior to Qualcomm, Matsumoto worked for Japanese conglomerate Itochu Corporation for 34 years, occupying various positions such as Senior VP of Itochu America's Electronics Division, and General Manager of Telecommunication and Multimedia Business. He was also Divisional VP of Space and Information Business Group at its Tokyo headquarters.

In 2013 and 2014, he served as a Special Visiting Professor for the Graduate School of Global Business at Meiji University.

www.ingramcontent.com/pod-product-compliance
Lightning Source LLC
Chambersburg PA
CBHW051233050326
40689CB00007B/902